Beyond Conventional Economics

Beyond Conventional Economics

The Limits of Rational Behaviour in Political Decision Making

Edited by

Giuseppe Eusepi

Professor of Public Finance, University of Rome 'La Sapienza', Italy

Alan Hamlin

Professor of Political Theory, University of Manchester, UK

Edward Elgar
Cheltenham, UK • Northampton, MA, USA

Published by
Edward Elgar Publishing Limited
Glensanda House
Montpellier Parade
Cheltenham
Glos GL50 1UA
UK

Edward Elgar Publishing, Inc.
136 West Street
Suite 202
Northampton
Massachusetts 01060
USA

A catalogue record for this book
is available from the British Library

ISBN-13: 978 1 84542 663 7
ISBN-10: 1 84542 663 0

Printed and bound in Great Britain by MPG Books Ltd, Bodmin, Cornwall

Contents

Figures and tables

FIGURES

TABLES

Contributors

James M. Buchanan, George Mason University, Fairfax, VA, USA

J.R. Clark, University of Tennessee at Chattanooga, TN, USA

Giuseppe Eusepi, University of Rome 'La Sapienza', Rome, Italy

Robert E. Goodin, RSSS, Australian National University, Canberra, Australia

Alan Hamlin, University of Manchester, Manchester, UK

Hartmut Kliemt, University of Duisburg, Duisburg, Germany

Dwight R. Lee, University of Georgia, Athens, GA, USA

Philip Pettit, Princeton University, Princeton, NJ, USA

Gordon Tullock, George Mason University, Arlington, VA, USA

Yong J. Yoon, George Mason University, Fairfax, VA, USA

Acknowledgements

This volume builds on the conference 'Beyond Conventional Economics. Studies in the Intellectual Development of Geoffrey Brennan', held in September 2004 at the Ministry of the Economy and Finance, Rome, Italy, organized by the European Center for the Study of Public Choice (ECSPC) and the Interdisciplinary Centre for International Economics (CIDEI) to honour and celebrate Geoffrey Brennan's 60th birthday.

We owe the ECSPC a debt for organizing the conference and giving us the chance to publish this volume. We also owe a debt to Capitalia Gruppo Bancario for generously funding the conference.

The ECSPC has already experienced a happy collaboration with Edward Elgar editorial staff and also on this occasion we appreciate their advice and support. Specifically we would like to thank Karen McCarthy, Alexandra Minton and Catherine Elgar.

Finally, Maria Delle Grotti, permanent secretary to the ECSPC, truly deserves our thanks for patiently assisting us in putting together the chapters that make up the present volume.

Giuseppe Eusepi
University of Rome 'La Sapienza'

Alan Hamlin
University of Manchester

Introduction

Giuseppe Eusepi and Alan Hamlin

As the title suggests, our intent in this volume is to give an account of the theoretical endeavours of those who seek to construct an approach to the analysis of political decision making that derives largely from economic theory but also recognizes and incorporates other areas of inquiry such as philosophy, more traditional political theory and psychology. This volume thus presents a critical examination of themes relevant to both human behaviour and economic and political institutions. But it offers more than a critique of the inadequacies underlying the conventional economic approach; it also offers a state-of-the-art tour of new paradigms challenging the dominant economic notion of the individual.

These issues are discussed in eight chapters by contributors from different academic backgrounds and covering topics conspicuously absent from conventional texts. But a further aspect of this collection is revealed by inspection of the set of contributors. While all are key actors in their own areas, an important fact that unites them is that they have all been Geoffrey Brennan's co-authors, and their chapters draw fresh attention to the topics and issues that characterize Brennan's intellectual development. Brennan was not the first in the Public Choice tradition to build links between economics, politics, philosophy and ethics. However, his work, and that of his co-authors, has been very influential in a number of areas and particularly in exploring our understanding of the limits of rational behaviour in political settings. This volume celebrates and plays tribute to that contribution.

Much space could be occupied in depicting Geoff Brennan's non-conventionality – not only as an economist choosing to write on subjects and using methods outside the mainstream of his discipline, but also as a person. Those who know Geoff would recognize him as a colourful and gregarious character. An economist, a semi-professional singer, and a philosopher *de facto*, Geoff is always willing to engage with debate regardless of its disciplinary origins and is always able to drive a point home with apt arguments and illustrations deriving from his multifaceted knowledge, but also with humour.

Brennan has been concerned to understand how ideas develop in order to add new dimensions to the mind-set of public choice scholars. While, in its early years, public choice was itself very much the challenger to the pre-vailing orthodoxy, its success in entering the mainstream of both econom-ics and politics has led to a new orthodoxy. Much of Geoff's work can be seen as continuing to challenge that emerging orthodoxy and expand the understanding of rational actor political theory. For example, in respect of methodological individualism, the standard public choice reference for methodological individualism is James Buchanan – who used it as the lens through which to analyse individuals' political behaviour. And even those who are hostile to such an epistemological tool have to admit the impact of the idea. But Buchanan's achievement is the starting point for Brennan, who has been concerned to refine and extend the idea of the individual that lies within the typical assumption of 'methodological individualism'. He assumes that the individual is an intellectual construction emanating from self-evaluation before being the elementary decision-making unit of exter-nal choice. So, the internal elements of the individual beyond the standard notions of desires and beliefs are the focus of considerable attention. Self-esteem is, for Brennan, a great shaping force for the individual, and inter-nal commitments or dispositions further extend the structure of the individual's internal constitution. Brennan's innovation, which underpins his novel view of individual behaviour in both economic and political spheres, challenges the structure of methodological individualism as we normally conceive it.

If one were to provide a bold outline of the essence of Brennan's scholar-ship no expression could be more appropriate than 'compound symmetry' – a phrase that suggests both the complexity of the individual and the need to view that complexity symmetrically when considering different social contexts. Although he is completely at one with the view that sees individu-als largely driven by egoism when choosing in the marketplace, such egoism is however only one component of the individual, one that is nuanced by, among other things, emotional relations to his fellow men, harking back to Adam Smith's notion of 'sympathy'. Brennan's individualism therefore mediates between egoism and sympathy. An individual is a composite con-sisting of several component motivations, to isolate any one is to commit an act of abstraction; they condition and qualify one another in ways that may yield rather different behaviours depending on the context. The notion of an individual wearing two hats: one of pure egoism for market choices, another of pure altruism for political choices is, for Brennan, a false opposition; the two perspectives must be fused into a whole. Yet, for Brennan, this is not simply a matter of coherence or internal consistency. It is deeply rooted in an approach to morality. Two components stand out in Brennan's work: limited rationality that goes well beyond likely conflicts of interest; and the moral need for a universal rule purged of all marks of discrimination, a rule that is valid for all individuals. Interestingly enough, whether Brennan acknowledges it or not (Brennan et al., 2001), this sort of nuanced Kantian categorical imperative is somewhat akin to Buchanan's 'relatively absolute absolutes'. It is exactly these 'relatively absolute absolutes' that are the hall-mark of the body of contractarian morality wherein the universal does not stand for eternal inalterability or 'absolutely absolute absolutes'. Since this kind of morality springs out of consensus, it is in principle binding on all contracting parties but is open to renegotiation – at least in principle.

A vivid example of the 'single-hat' approach can be found in *Democracy and Decision* (1993), written with Loren Lomasky, which marks a crucial turning point in departing from traditional analysis in public choice. With respect to electoral politics, Brennan and Lomasky charge that orthodox public choice theory places undue emphasis on the interest-based theory of voting behaviour. They develop the concept of expressive voting, and reach the conclusion that electoral choice and market choice are radically different, but for reasons that stem from an integrated view of the rational individuals involved in both forms of choice.

Over the course of his career to date, Geoff Brennan has written on a wide range of topics only some of which are reflected in the chapters of this book. However, the broad themes of his work – the challenge to the con-ventional, the emphasis on the rich internal structure of the individual, and the focus on the complex interactions between individuals and institutions are reflected here.

The first part, 'Building democracy: aspects of voting and vigilance', opens with a chapter by Alan Hamlin entitled 'Political dispositions and dispositional politics' which builds on recent joint work with Geoff Brennan in arguing for a dispositional account of aspects of individual motivation. This chapter tackles the idea of a dispositional account of political motiv-ation directly to clarify and extend the discussion of the nature of a dispo-sition; suggest a typology of dispositions; discuss the relationship between dispositions, desires and beliefs; comment of the importance of disposi-tions in political settings; and say something about the case of multiple dis-positions. The chapter also includes a discussion of the relationship between the idea of dispositional motivation and the idea of expressive motivation.

In Chapter 2, 'Expressive voting: how special interests enlist their victims as political allies', J.R. Clark and Dwight R. Lee pick up the theme of expres-sive motivation in voting and introduce interest groups into the analysis. Interest groups act instrumentally and Clark and Lee argue that sophisti-cated interest groups will pitch their communication with individuals on the basis of an understanding of the distinction between their interest and their expressive concerns. Thus, encouragement of expressive voting by interest groups may be the first step in victimizing members of the general public. In effect, voters are enlisted as political allies of those who seek to exploit their expressive concerns. Nevertheless, Clark and Lee conclude that expressive voting can provide voters with their best hope for imposing discipline on their political agents.

In Chapter 3, Giuseppe Eusepi tackles the fundamental question of *quis custodiet ipsos custodes* in his chapter entitled 'Who shall keep the keepers themselves? On the moral foundations of the separation of powers'. The author argues that the classic problem is typical of separated powers and alien to either anarchy or absolutism. Careful attention is paid to how the institutional environment moulds the different guises the problem might have. Drawing upon work by Geoff Brennan, the author elaborates the concept of compound symmetry. Eusepi's portrait of constitutional courts reveals how difficult it is to have a third party as the ultimate guardian or keeper. He attempts to demystify the role of constitutional courts in Western democracies, and provides a reply to the often-asked question: 'Is the constitutional court, which has been empowered to keep the keepers, an impartial institution that prevents dictatorial solutions?' To answer this question he focuses on the Italian Constitutional Court and shows how the body that was originally designated to control the government ends up by making the *quis custodiet ipsos custodes* problem a perennial one. He concludes by suggesting the possible devices that can be introduced to limit rent-seeking activities by the government and the measures to be put in place to prevent the judges of the Court from behaving as informal agents of the government.

Part I ends with a chapter by Gordon Tullock entitled 'A bouquet of democracies'. Here Tullock displays his range as a historian of ancient and modern democracies to illustrate the variety of practices that fall within the scope of democracy. In his view, democracy is not a specific type or form of government, but a collection or bouquet of types with rather different characteristics. Such a bouquet includes, for example, countries in which voting is compulsory (as in Australia) as well as countries in which voting is a right but not a duty. Compulsory voting ensures that the voting majority is also descriptive of the real majority, but compulsion may also have impacts on how well informed voting might be. There is similar variety in a number of other areas – for example the nature and extent of the franchise. Though admitting that in countries where citizens are legally required to vote the outcome reflects more faithfully voters' preferences than that achieved in those countries where voting is voluntary, Tullock argues that compulsory voting may be perceived as oppressive. After considering a variety of democracies, Tullock finally addresses the important question of whether organizations such as the United Nations can be seen as democratic institutions. Here he argues that the UN cannot be defined as a democratic institution since votes are cast by governments, which in the majority of cases are themselves not democratic, and not by citizens.

The second part of the collection, 'Searching for stability in democracy', opens with Chapter 5 by James M. Buchanan and Yong J. Yoon, entitled 'Subjective evaluation of alternatives in individual voting choice'. For the authors, the individual's primitive preference ordering is the benchmark and base of the conventional analysis of voting behaviour. In market exchange, maximizing behaviour implies that choices mirror this preference ordering. In collective choice contexts, such as voting, this linkage is not present. The ability of the individual to order differences, a property of subjective cardinal utility, does not add explanatory power to market behaviour. Such ability becomes relevant, however, in explaining individual behaviour in collective or political settings. The argument is focussed on demonstrating that disconnects emerge between primitive orderings and revealed voting when the individual is acknowledged to be able to order differences and to make predictions about the voting behaviour of others. The authors criticize the cardinal version of utilitarian theory that has dominated economic analysis before Robbins, and as revived by the 'new' welfare economics. In developing their criticism, Buchanan and Yoon draw the contrast between economic markets, characterized by individual choices, and political markets where these 'choices' do not produce direct consequences due to the existence of public goods.

In Chapter 6, Robert E. Goodin writes on 'Truth, justice and democracy', asking the basic question of whether democracy contributes toward the pursuit of either truth or justice. The discussion revolves around two theorems – the Condorcet jury theorem, and the majority rule theorem – one of which (Condorcet) is related to the idea of truth, while the other is related to the idea of justice, interpreted as the impartial satisfaction of preferences. The strategy of the chapter is then to analyse the extent to which these two theorems pull against each other in specifying properties of democracy. Goodin concludes that while democracy can promote both truth and justice in some circumstances – particularly in individualistic societies where each voter is seen as an isolated example of *homo economicus* – there are other circumstances in which democracy may fail to track either truth or justice, and still others where democracy may be just but may not yield the truth. More generally, Goodin exposes the more fine-grained nature of the relationships between the behaviour of individuals, the institutional structures of democracy, and the normative properties associated with democracy.

In Chapter 7 on 'Error-dependent norms', Philip Pettit pursues the puzzling cases of social norms that are supported precisely by errors made by individuals. Pettit begins by reviewing the nature and definition of social norms to draw out the idea that norms are supported by patterns of approval and disapproval in the population – or by beliefs about patterns of approval and disapproval. This leads to the possibility that these beliefs may be erroneous. Everyone may believe that everyone else approves of X, while in fact no-one actually approves of X, but acts as if they do out of a desire to conform. More subtly, even if everyone is correct in their beliefs about approval, they may be mistaken in believing that this approval is important in motivating behaviour – that is, they may be wrong to believe that others internalize the norm. Pettit goes on to argue that error-dependent norms are not just a logical curiosity, but may play a significant role in explicating a variety of social behaviour – and that the normative impact of such norms can be either positive or negative.

The volume ends with a chapter by Hartmut Kliemt entitled 'The world is a table. Economic philosophy stated flatly in terms of rows, columns and cells'. He starts from the Buchananesque observation that, properly speaking, there cannot be 'social choice' since individuals rather than societies make choices – so that 'social choices' must be seen to emerge from individual choices. Using Pattanaik's recent re-evaluation of the social choice approach, a deliberational and an institutional variant are exemplified by discussions of Sen's paradox of liberalism. Where Sen must deal with the 'liberal nature' of the evaluation of games and the rank ordering of whole game forms, the normative constitutional political economist discusses the more or less 'liberal' character of the rules of the games that are ranked. But, as suspected by Bergson and Little, social choice theory must be about axiology rather than choice.

One is, however, left with the impression that in Kliemt's scholarly analysis there is a general and implicit assumption of property rights – an issue that has prompted a good deal of discussion in the study of liberalism. In order to exemplify the argument, Kliemt constructs a two-person game in a context where rows, columns and cells represent the choice options available to two individuals. In this setting neither individual has the power to choose desired outcomes since neither of them can determine the final result (the cell) – each can only choose his or her own action. Kliemt's discussion points to a sense in which individuals may attempt to behave concertedly rather than merely strategically – so that individuals in some way incorporate aspects of the social in their own decision making.

Kliemt's retelling of Sen's liberal paradox story about who is entitled to read *Lady Chatterley's Lover* casts new light on the debate, and tells us that not only does liberalism prevent paradoxes from emerging, but it allows the solution of further problems provided that all individuals are permitted to exchange property within a system of defined property rights.

These chapters, taken together, offer a range of novel insights into the limits of rational behaviour in political decision making, but also offer strategies for exploring these limits that promise rewards across a range of issues. If a hallmark of Geoff Brennan's work is that it combines wide-ranging interests attracted by puzzles and paradoxes with a deep commitment to the analysis of the interaction between the individual and society, then these chapters seem to us to be very much in the Brennan tradition.

REFERENCES

Brennan, Geoffrey and Loren Lomasky (1993), *Democracy and Decision. The Pure Theory of Electoral Preference*, Cambridge, UK and New York, USA: Cambridge University Press.

Brennan, Geoffrey, Hartmut Kliemt and Robert T. Tollison (eds) (2001), *Method and Morals in Constitutional Economics: Essays in Honor of James, M. Buchanan*, Berlin: Springer-Verlag.

PART I

Building democracy: aspects of voting and vigilance

1. Political dispositions and dispositional politics

Alan Hamlin

INTRODUCTION

First, a caricature of a 'typical economist'[1]: he (the typical economist is male) works with a very basic Humean model of individual rationality and motivation that defines a rational action or choice in any given setting as that action/choice, of those actions/choices that are available, that best serves the individual's desires, given the individual's beliefs. The understanding of the idea of desires is couched in terms of preferences and their satisfaction, but also in terms of interests – indeed desires, preferences and interests will often be taken as fully synonymous. Preferences provide the mainspring to rational action, are fully consistent with the individual's interests, are inscrutable (*de gustibus non est disputandum*), and operate on one level. Much of the work of this typical economist in recent years has been focussed on the analysis of the implications of variations in the informational environment in which the individual operates, with uncertainty and asymmetric information being key ideas. While there has been some concern with models of bounded rationality, there has been comparatively little attention to other issues associated with motivation, preferences, desires and interests.

This 'typical' approach to economics has been evident in the recent burgeoning literature on political economics, where the mainstream economic approach is applied to issues of politics and political institutions.[2] Here the focus has been very much on the political life of *homo economicus* – with the fully rational individual with preferences that are identical to interest at the heart of the analysis.

But not all economists are 'typical'.[3] Even a slightly richer version of the Humean model[4] would allow of distinctions between an individual's passions, sentiments, moral judgements, character traits, will, identity and so on, that are lost within the 'typical' economist's schema. My purpose here is not to provide an interpretation of Hume (although I consider the account that I offer broadly Humean), but rather to focus on one particular

3

extension to the typical economist's model which includes the idea of dispositions as a potentially significant element of the motivational makeup of individuals – an element that plays a role that is in some ways complementary to the role of simple preferences and which builds on earlier work with Geoff Brennan.[5]

A specific benefit of the more detailed consideration of individual motivation relates to the potential disconnect between the descriptive or analytic aspirations of rational choice political theory on the one hand and its normative aspirations on the other. As Christiano (2004) notes, the strict adherence to a narrowly self-interested rationality threatens a 'basic structural determinism' under which the normative aims of rational choice theory may be undermined, at least to a significant degree. While we do not accept all of Christiano's discussion, we are certainly in agreement that there is an important issue here. In our view, the most promising way out of the potential impasse (or, more accurately, the most promising way to reduce the extent of the tension between the normative and the descriptive aspects of the theory) is to develop a more nuanced account of the individual's motivational structure that is both more descriptively accurate and more connected to normative concerns. The move to recognize dispositions and place them in the landscape of political behaviour is one step along this path.

My title picks out two rather different perspectives – one focussed on specifically political dispositions, which includes an argument as to why the idea of dispositions may be more relevant in the political domain than in the domain of the market; the other focussed on the implications for our understanding of politics that arise from recognizing the dispositional input. The next section seeks to be explicit about the idea of a disposition and to identify the role that dispositions play in relation to preferences. I then develop the discussion of dispositions by contrasting the theme of dispositional motivation with the theme of expressive motivation and present the argument that dispositions may be particularly significant in the political domain. In the following section I discuss the two particular dispositions that Geoff Brennan and I have been interested in, in order to draw out more general issues. The final section stands in place of conclusions and returns to the distinction between political dispositions and dispositional politics.

DISPOSITIONS

While dispositions feature prominently in a wide range of philosophical literatures, they are rarely the centre of attention.[6] Often the word is used simply to identify an intentional state, without any very specific implications for the further properties of that intentional state. Where dispositions are at centre stage, the idea of a disposition is most often related to the idea of higher order preferences. For example, Lewis (1989) suggests that something is a value if and only we are disposed, under ideal circumstances, to value it, where the disposition in question is a matter of second order desire.[7] This conception clearly links to the earlier work on higher order preferences by Jeffrey (1974) and particularly Frankfurt (1971); although these articles do not themselves employ the word disposition systematically. Frankfurt, for example, speaks of second order volitions that are a particular class of second order desires such that the individual wants a particular desire to be his will. Holding such volitions is argued to be constitutive of personhood and moral agency. I will retain a link between dispositions and higher order desires, although I do not identify a disposition directly with a second order desire – rather I will suggest that a disposition is a piece of motivational apparatus that may be influenced by first or higher order desires in the long term, and which operates to condition or govern first order desires and behaviour in the short term.

Roughly, a disposition is a kind of commitment that might be identified with a temperament, temper, inclination, trait, commitment, mind-set, or tendency. One might be disposed to tell the truth, or one might be of a cautious disposition, but, if so, this would not necessarily mean that one always told the truth, or avoided all avoidable risks. A disposition – whatever its specific content – is not an absolute determinant or guarantor of behaviour in the relevant domain. Nevertheless, a disposition does carry some motivational force that may modify, and sometimes dominate, what might otherwise be desired and chosen. A truthful disposition will reduce the number of lies told relative to the situation in which the disposition was absent but all other desires are identical.

A disposition, therefore, lies somewhere between the extremes of a hardwired model of determinism in which behaviour is fully committed and independent of the consideration of desires, and Frankfurt's 'wanton' behaviour in which individuals follow each fleeting whim or want without any restraint. Of course, the range between these two extremes is considerable, covering all forms of habitual behaviour, rules of thumb, personal and social norms of behaviour, and so on. I will not attempt to categorize all of the possibilities, or to provide a taxonomy of the spectrum. I simply note the family resemblance across this range and stipulate that a disposition occupies a place on this spectrum such that the strength of the commitment relative to simple first order desires is significant, but not necessarily overpowering. This formulation entails a certain structural relationship between dispositions and desires. Dispositions might be said to govern desires or decisions in the same way that a convention governs behaviour over some relevant domain, or the rules of a game govern behaviour within that game. Compliance with the convention, rule or disposition is not automatic, and may be withheld in some cases, but the existence of the convention, rule or disposition is at least influential. This link between the idea of a disposition and the idea of an internal constitutional rule[8] is one that provides a clear connection between the interest in, and analysis of, dispositions and the constitutional political economy approach to politics more generally.

The content of a disposition may also shape its form. The examples already given of a disposition to tell the truth, or to be cautious, might be termed *general conditioning dispositions* in that they apply, to a greater or lesser extent, to a wide range of decision contexts and domains. Other dispositions may be more selective, with relevance to specific domains of behaviour – for example the commitment to be a vegetarian or to support a specific sports team might be described in terms of a disposition that is cultivated and which may from time to time conflict with particular desires. Such dispositions might be classed as *specific conditioning dispositions*.

A third type of disposition is concerned with identifying the mode of decision making itself, rather than influencing decisions within a mode. In an earlier discussion of dispositions, Geoff Brennan and I focussed on this type of disposition. To quote:

> A disposition picks out a particular mode of decision making which may then be applied to the choice among possible actions; a disposition involves a procedure or mechanism that allows a set of decisions on actions to be bundled together and made according to a particular rule. Thus a disposition identifies both a class of choice situations and a choice rule, and involves the application of the specified rule in the specified situations.
>
>   Seen in this way, self-interested calculation over actions (together with some specification of the class of actions to which it should apply) is itself a disposition: the disposition of rational egoism. This disposition tells you to take that action which, of those actions that are available to you, makes your life go best for you (i.e. maximises your expected lifetime pay-off). But the disposition of rational egoism is not necessarily the disposition that will make your life go best for you. Your expected lifetime pay-off may be larger if you were to have a different disposition. If this is true, the disposition of rational egoism (the *homo economicus* disposition) is self-defeating in Parfit's sense; and it would be in your own interest to choose a different disposition if only that were possible. (Brennan and Hamlin, 2000, 35–6)

This class of dispositions might be termed *modal dispositions*.[9]

Dispositions, on this account, are distinct from both desires (of whatever order) and beliefs. Dispositions provide the framework within which desires interact with beliefs in generating decisions or actions. It might be suggested that dispositions are a variety of second order desires – but I would resist this suggestion on the grounds that while one might have second order desires that relate to dispositions (indicting the desirability of having a particular disposition, say) this is not the same thing as the disposition itself. Similarly, it might be argued that a disposition is a variety of belief (for example the belief that morality requires particular actions), but again I would resist this suggestion on the grounds that a disposition plays a role that is rather more specific than a belief – it commits the individual in particular ways that the holding of a belief does not. Beliefs of a certain sort may be a necessary precondition or input to a disposition, but that are not the whole story.

Perhaps the most plausible suggestion is that a disposition is a form of product of a belief and a desire – so that, for example, a moral disposition might be formed of a combination of a belief that morality requires particular actions, and the desire to act as morality requires. And this formulation gets close to the suggestion here. Close, but not quite there. What this formulation still misses is the extent of the commitment involved in a disposition. The combined belief–desire account would still locate the moral motivation at the level of a desire – in the example used, the desire to act as morality requires. And this desire would sit alongside other desires which might point to other actions. There is then the further question of how the individual decides in the face of a complex belief–desire context. The point that I would stress about a disposition is that it implies some structure to decision making rather than simply providing another desire–belief input to decision making.

So far, I have spoken only about the content of a disposition and the position of dispositions in the motivational machinery. I now turn briefly to consider the source and evolution of dispositions. Dispositions may arise and evolve under a variety of causal influences. Some of these influences may lie outside of the control of the individual. I make no claim that all dispositions can be fully determined by the will or behaviour of the individual concerned, even in the long term (clearly the idea of a disposition as a relatively fixed part of the individual's motivational apparatus rules out the short-term control of one's own dispositions). However, I do claim that many relevant dispositions – of each of the three types identified above – can be at least influenced by the individual (and, indeed, by other individuals – parents, advisors, friends, and so on).

It seems clear that some dispositions of the specific conditioning kind can be explicitly chosen and reinforced by behaviour. Commitment strategies such as vegetarianism or adopting an exercise regime are examples of such dispositions. But it is equally clear that the choice and reinforcement of such a disposition is not a trivial matter – the fate of most New Year resolutions and the difficulties of giving up smoking remind us that dispositional choice and reinforcement behaviour are costly in terms of other desires denied. In this regard, I suggest that more general and modal dispositions are also susceptible to choice and reinforcement, at least to some extent. We can resolve to be more cautious, or more truthful, or more rational in our financial decision making. And our resolve can, at least sometimes, be translated into modified dispositions through both efforts of will and reinforcing behaviour.

In Brennan and Hamlin (1995) we offered a very simple model of dispositional choice in which individuals choose on a once-and-for-all basis between two dispositions that commit the individual to different modes of decision making. The disposition, once chosen, influences the performance of the individual in different social roles, and imperfect selection mechanisms attempt to ensure that persons of a given disposition are matched to appropriate roles. The main point of this model – aside from illustrating dispositional choice itself – was to indicate the manner in which institutional arrangements might themselves influence dispositional choice.

Just as, in simple market models, the consumption and production choices made by firms and individuals are influenced by institutional factors – regulations, taxes, and so on – so the choice of disposition (to the extent that dispositions are chosen) will be influenced by institutional and constitutional factors. And, because of this, the question of institutional design takes on additional dimensions. The most obvious of these is that institutions must be designed which recognize and work with motivational and dispositional heterogeneity. But the dynamic dimension of institutional design may be just as important, if less obvious, than the heterogeneity dimension. Rather than designing institutions that operate well in the presence of individuals with fixed motivations, institutions can also influence the evolution of dispositions and motivations. Of course, this additional dimension should not be overemphasized; the evolution of dispositions will be slow and partial at best, and the more immediate task of institutions may always seem to dominate. But nevertheless, there may be particular issues, or particular aspects of social institutions, where the impact via dispositions may be expected to be significant.

Clearly, dispositions may be relevant to almost all aspects of behaviour, and I have given a range of examples to illustrate this. However, my focus here is on political dispositions – by which I mean dispositions that are particularly relevant to the domain of politics, rather than on dispositions where the content of the disposition might be judged 'political' in some other sense. I do not intend to claim that a dispositional account of motivation is uniquely relevant to politics – only that it is relevant to politics and that there may be particular features of the evolution of political dispositions and of the operation of democratic politics that allow us to say something about the likely impact of shifting from an account of democratic politics that operates in terms of interests and first order desires to one that recognizes the potential importance of dispositions. The first step here concerns the relationship between dispositional and expressive motivation.

DISPOSITIONAL AND EXPRESSIVE MOTIVATION

It is useful to distinguish between dispositional aspects of motivation and expressive aspects of motivation, not only because the distinction can help to clarify both ideas, but also because the two aspects each occupy an important place in the approach adopted in various Brennan and Hamlin papers and laid out here.[10]

The key to understanding the expressive aspect of motivation is to recognize that expressive desires are first order desires like any other, but that they generally become significant in influencing action only in circumstances where the individual's action is of relatively low consequential significance. It is not that the expressive desires are irrelevant in other circumstances, or somehow excluded from consideration, but just that they will generally be overwhelmed by more standard instrumental desires. In one sense, the recognition of expressive preferences is not so much a recognition of a different category of desires, but more the recognition of a set of desires that are normally overlooked simply because they are insignificant in the settings that economists normally focus on – settings where individuals are decisive and their decisions carry direct consequences. Of course, in another sense, there is something distinctive about the set of expressive desires – the fact that their satisfaction can be achieved without necessarily involving particular further consequences. Thus I can satisfy my (expressive) desire to voice my opinion that Z should happen, without any necessary requirement that Z should actually happen. It is, in this case, the simple expression of the opinion that matters.

The leading example of expressive behaviour is provided by voting in large-scale democratic elections – where the probability of any individual's vote being decisive is so low as to free the individual from any instrumental reasons for voting (or for voting in any particular way), thereby leaving expressive desires – those that can be satisfied by the act of voting itself regardless of the outcome of the election – as the desires that will determine whether and how the individual will vote.

Dispositions operate in a quite different part of the motivational landscape, picking up the degree of commitment to a particular desire or mode of action, rather than identifying a type or desire or a subset of desires. In this way, one might identify the possibility of either expressive or instrumental dispositions. And indeed, that is part of the intention here. But the fact that dispositions and expressive motivations are logically independent of each other does not imply that there are not further connections.

I argue that the same logic that promotes expressive considerations over instrumental considerations in the context of large-scale political and public decision making also tends to promote dispositions over simple desires or interests. Just as the individually inconsequential nature of public choices such as voting shifts the relative prices of acting on expressive rather than instrumental desires, so it reduces the price of acting according to your disposition rather than your first order desires.

Recall that a disposition – of whichever type – does not guarantee a particular decision or action, the commitment is not absolute. Dispositions will be more likely to be effective when alternative pressures on decision making are low. And the most obvious source of alternative pressures on decision making is instrumental desires. So, if the choice situation is framed in such a way as to background the relevance of instrumental desires, the disposition will be more likely to be effective. In the private context, if you are committed (but not absolutely committed) to vegetarianism the best chance of the commitment being effective is to avoid situations which offer tempting non-vegetarian meals and limited vegetarian options. In the public context, if you are a committed (but not absolutely committed) supporter of a particular policy your support is more likely to be effective if you are asked to vote on it rather than to take individual responsibility for a decision.

Thus, I suggest, democratic politics will typically provide citizens with an arena in which their dispositions and expressive desires are elicited rather than their direct first order desires or interests. This, in itself, is neither a good thing nor a bad thing. Everything will depend upon the particular content of the relevant dispositions and expressive desires. But this does serve to throw attention onto the analysis of the likely content of dispositions and expressive desires and onto the impact that the distinction between dispositions and expressive desires, on the one hand, and instrumental desires and interests, on the other hand, may have on the operation of political and social institutions.

VIRTUE AND CONSERVATISM

The two dispositions that Geoff Brennan and I have discussed in our recent work are the virtuous disposition and the conservative disposition. These dispositions have structural similarities and differences that are informative. I will sketch each in turn.

The virtuous disposition is argued (Brennan and Hamlin (2000) particularly Chapters 2 and 3) to derive in the manner briefly sketched in the last section – that is, to reflect an underlying first order desire to act as morality requires, together with a particular belief about what morality requires. The shift from the level of a moral desire to a virtuous disposition is then argued in terms of a modal disposition. In brief, the argument is that a fully instrumentally rational attempt to make life go as well as possible is potentially self-defeating in the sense that the adoption of a standard rationality calculus will systematically achieve worse results than an available alternative mode of decision making – one which adopts a greater commitment to morality or virtue. The logic here is essentially similar to the logic of the prisoner's dilemma in that the prisoner's dilemma identifies a situation in which the instrumental rationality of each prisoner prevents them from reaching an outcome that would be mutually advantageous. Thus the adoption of a virtuous disposition (to the extent that a virtuous disposition can be adopted) is argued to be a rational piece of self-management that pays off when evaluated with respect to the full set of underlying desires.

By contrast, the conservative disposition (Brennan and Hamlin, 2004) is a disposition that grants the status quo a normative authority by virtue of its being the status quo. Contrary to the case of the virtuous disposition, the conservative disposition does not reflect an underlying first order desire to do as conservatism requires. This is, in part, because we regard conservatism to be a position that qualifies substantive political goals, rather than identifies specifically conservative goals; thus we think it most appropriate to use the word conservative adjectivally – a conservative liberal, or a conservative utilitarian, rather than simply a conservative. But also, and more importantly, because we analyse conservatism in terms that emphasize its basis in an attitude to two forms of uncertainty – the uncertainty associated with policy outcomes, and the deeper uncertainty associated with the difficulty of identifying appropriate political ideals. Thus, the conservative position is, on our account, largely a matter of taking feasibility seriously in recognizing the general properties of consequential evaluation in the presence of uncertainties. But the conservative disposition is a means of making this position effective:

> Even economists are familiar with the thought that there is a distinction between justification and motivation. The market produces the benign outcomes that are claimed for it by 'invisible' means. In other words, the properties that serve to justify market outcomes are not aspects that necessarily motivate any of the agents whose actions produce those outcomes. In the same way here, what works to motivate conservatives may not be the same as what justifies conservatism. The conservative disposition – an intuitive suspicion of all grand schemes, an intrinsic affection for things as they are, an inclination to be reconciled to one's general situation and perhaps strongly self-identified with it, a tendency to evaluate policies and reforms in terms of 'disaster avoidance' rather than utopian aspiration – may be what motivates conservatives, as a matter of descriptive fact.

> More to the point, it may be good for those who recognise the intellectual force of the conservative position to positively cultivate that particular disposition. (Brennan and Hamlin, 2004)

Thus, in terms of our earlier typology, we regard the conservative disposition as a general conditioning disposition – a lens or filter through which the world is seen, rather than a mode of decision making.

These two dispositions differ, then, in several important respects: they are of different types – one a modal disposition and one a general conditioning disposition; they carry different relationships to underlying desires – one building on a first order desire, the other not. But despite these differences they both operate to modify the behaviour of the individual in a manner that will be particularly important in the political domain.

Of course, there are many possible dispositions, including many possible political dispositions, and any individual may be characterized by a number of political dispositions. In particular, there is no reason to suppose that an individual cannot be both virtuous and conservative by disposition. Of course, the possibility of multiple dispositions that may each be relevant to a particular circumstance raises new issues. It is no longer the case that we are simply concerned with the tension between a particular commitment or disposition and the range of relevant desires, but also with the tensions between distinct commitments or dispositions.

I will not attempt any general discussion of the resolution of such tensions here; rather I will make a few comments that I hope may prove suggestive, based in part on the two particular dispositions under discussion. First, whether or not there is conflict between dispositions is a matter that is contingent on the particular circumstances. If two (or more) dispositions were never in conflict in any possible situation, then it would be possible to formally combine those dispositions and treat them as one. On the other hand, if two dispositions conflicted in all possible situations it is difficult to see how a single individual could genuinely be said to hold both dispositions simultaneously. In some circumstances virtue and conservatism will point to the same action or decision, in other circumstances their implications will differ. If the dispositions align in terms of their implied actions there is no further issue of major significance – the relevant action is doubly recommended. If they differ, then there are several issues to consider. The first relates to the types of the dispositions. If, as in this example, the dispositions are of different types, this may indicate the manner of the resolution of the conflict between them. Specifically, the conservative disposition indicates a particular stance toward evaluating options that biases one toward the status quo, whereas the virtuous disposition puts in place a mode of decision making that privileges moral considerations over self-interested ones in certain circumstances. Even if these two do not obviously point to the same decision or action in some particular setting (that is, even if the action that morality requires is not in the relevant sense the status quo) they may be procedurally compatible in the sense that the conservative evaluations of alternative options (including the status quo) may be used as inputs to the virtuous mode of decision making. This will provide a status quo bias to the virtuous calculus in such a way that the resultant decision or action will be likely to depart from that which would be chosen either by an individual who was simply conservative or by an individual who was simply virtuous, but this is a perfectly coherent approach to what it might mean to be 'conservatively virtuous'. In this way, we see that while there may seem to be conflict between dispositions in the sense that each disposition taken separately would pick out a different decision is a specific context, the dispositions themselves may contain the resolution to this apparent conflict revealing a deeper compatibility between the dispositions.

Not all conflicts may be so easily resolved. But it is surely reasonable to expect the dispositions of a single individual to be coherent in the sense that, under the broad range of circumstances that might be considered normal, the dispositions do not generally suffer from deep conflict. Indeed, if an individual's dispositions give rise to frequent deep conflicts one might suggest that this indicates a pathology in the individual that might be approached via the questioning and review of the dispositions adopted.

CONCLUSION

In much of our recent work, Geoff Brennan and I have seen a more detailed attention to the motivational structure of individuals as an important step toward enriching the rational actor analysis of political decision making and of political institutions. I believe that the idea of dispositions as motivational structures that govern and partially commit the (first order) desires of individuals sits alongside the recognition of the more expressive elements of desire to provide what we would regard as a considerably stronger starting point for political analysis than that provided by the stripped down motivational structure preferred by the 'typical' economist caricatured at the outset of this chapter.

But the proof of the pudding lies in the eating. It is only if the model of motivation that embraces the dispositional and the expressive generates additional or different implications and understandings to those derived from the more stripped down model, that the exercise is worthwhile. We believe that the extended model does help us to understand a range of political behaviour and a rage of institutional phenomena, but this particular pudding requires much further tasting.

I want, finally, to return to two themes – one relating to the relationship between descriptive and normative political theory, the other relating to the distinction between political dispositions and dispositional politics. In pulling these themes together, I want to suggest that the dispositional approach has the potential to enrich the motivational landscape in a way that is particularly relevant to democratic politics on the understanding that dispositions provide a sort of internal, personal 'constitution', and that democratic politics provides a particularly fertile ground in which dispositions can flourish; so that political dispositions are both a descriptively plausible part of the motivational structure of individuals and likely to be effective in real political contexts. But I also want to suggest that the study of politics has to adjust to take account of such dispositions. Dispositional politics allows much clearer connections between descriptive and normative political theory by raising the possibility of normatively driven dispositions being significant determinants of individual political behaviour. But dispositional politics also sets different challenges to, for example, institutional designers or reformers. If rational agents can be understood as voting their dispositions (or their expressive opinions) rather than their interests, our normative understanding of the operational properties of political institutions must change and so may our institutional prescriptions. The recognition of the expressive and dispositional aspects of political motivation does not just deepen our analysis of political behaviour and institutions; it will also provide us with different diagnoses of political failures, and different institutional remedies.

But my purpose here has not been to detail these diagnoses and remedies. Rather, I have sought to clarify and extend the discussion of the nature of a disposition; suggest a typology of dispositions; discuss the relationship between dispositions, desires and beliefs; comment of the importance of dispositions in political settings; and say something about the case of multiple dispositions. While this is not a jointly authored chapter in the detail of its attribution, it is essentially joint in that it reflects my understanding of what a considerable part of my work with Geoff Brennan has been about over recent years. Of course, all of this needs considerable further work, and this is work that takes us well beyond conventional economics.

NOTES

1. It must be said that the typical economist caricatured here is less dominant than was the case twenty or even ten years ago. Nevertheless, he is hardly an endangered species. While

     many economists would acknowledge the limitations of the approach caricatured in principle, it still dominates the profession in practice.

2. See, for example, Persson and Tabellini (2000).
3. For recent examples see Frey (1997a, b), Le Grand (2003), Besley (forthcoming).
4. See, for example, Baier (1991), Bricke (1996), Sugden (1986).
5. Particularly, Brennan and Hamlin (1995, 1998, 2000, 2004).
6. For example, the *Routledge Encyclopedia of Philosophy* includes over 140 articles that include the word 'disposition', but there is no article devoted to the idea of a disposition, and none of the articles offers a definition or extended discussion of the idea of a disposition. Indeed, it is clear that the word is used to mean rather different things by different authors.
7. See Copp (1993) and Harman (1993) for a modified account and a critique.
8. The connection between internal personal constitutions and political constitutions appears, for example, in Brennan and Buchanan (1985).
9. I make no claim that these three types of dispositions exhaust the possibilities.
10. For detailed analysis of expressive aspects of democratic politics see Brennan and Lomasky (1993) and Brennan and Hamlin (1998, 2000).

REFERENCES

Baier, A.C. (1991), *A Progress of Sentiments: Reflections on Hume's 'Treatise'*, Cambridge, Mass.: Harvard University Press.

Besley, T. (forthcoming), *Principled Agents*, Oxford: Oxford University Press.

Brennan, G. and Buchanan, J.M. (1985), *The Reason of Rules*, Cambridge: Cambridge University Press.

Brennan, G. and Hamlin, A. (1995), 'Economizing on Virtue', *Constitutional Political Economy*, **6** (1), 35–6.

Brennan, G. and Hamlin, A. (1998), 'Expressive Voting and Electoral Equilibrium', *Public Choice*, **95**, 149–75.

Brennan, G. and Hamlin, A. (2000), *Democratic Devices and Desires*, Cambridge: Cambridge University Press.

Brennan, G. and Hamlin, A. (2004), 'Analytic Conservatism', *British Journal of Political Science*, **34** (4), 675–91.

Brennan, G. and Lomasky, L. (1993), *Democracy and Decisions: The Pure Theory of Electoral Preference*, New York: Cambridge University Press.

Bricke, J. (1996), *Hume's Moral Psychology*, Oxford: Oxford University Press.

Christiano, T. (2004), 'Is Normative Rational Choice Theory Self-Defeating?', *Ethics*, **115**, 122–41.

Copp, D. (1993), 'Reason and Needs', in R.G. Frey and C.W. Morris (eds), *Value, Welfare and Morality*, Cambridge: Cambridge University Press, pp. 112–37.

Frankfurt, H. (1971), 'Freedom of the Will and the Concept of a Person', *Journal of Philosophy*, **68** (1), 5–20.

Frey, B. (1997a), 'A Constitution for Knaves Crowds Out Civic Virtues', *Economic Journal*, **107**, 1043–53.

Frey, B. (1997b), *Not Just for the Money*, Cheltenham, UK, and Brookfield, US: Edward Elgar.

Harman, G. (1993), 'Desired Desires', in R.G. Frey and C.W. Morris (eds), *Value, Welfare and Morality*, Cambridge: Cambridge University Press, pp. 138–57.

Jeffrey, R. (1974), 'Preference among Preferences', *Journal of Philosophy*, **68**, 377–91.

Le Grand, J. (2003), *Motivation, Agency and Public Policy*, Oxford: Oxford University Press.

Lewis, D. (1989), 'Dispositional Theories of Value', *Proceedings of the Aristotelian Society*, **63**, 113–37.

Persson, T. and Tabellini, G. (2000), *Political Economics*, Cambridge, Mass.: MIT Press.

Sugden, R. (1986), *The Economics of Rights, Co-operation and Welfare*, Oxford: Basil Blackwell.

2. Expressive voting: how special interests enlist their victims as political allies

J.R. Clark and Dwight R. Lee

INTRODUCTION

Often the most powerful insights are not the needles in a haystack, but the proverbial $20 bills that lie in plain view on the sidewalk for decades without being picked up. This is the case, subject to a qualification, with expressive voting. Brennan and Lomasky spotted the money on the sidewalk and scooped it up with their 1993 book *Democracy and Decisions: The Pure Theory of Electoral Preference*. Until then economists (even public choice economists) could be forgiven for arguing that voters cast their votes for politicians and policies that they believed best served their private interests. True, rational apathy might keep them from going to the polls, and rational ignorance might cause them to mistakenly vote against their interest if they got to the polls, but once in the voting booth, voters intended to support outcomes that benefited them and to oppose outcomes that harmed them.

Brennan and Lomasky's work is related to, but takes us beyond, the insights of rational apathy and ignorance that had been well known since the work of Downs (1957). Rational apathy and ignorance result from the low (minuscule in state and national elections) probability that the outcome of an election will be decided by one vote. Why go to the trouble of voting if the probability that your vote will be decisive is indistinguishable from zero, or if you do vote, why bother to become well informed? It is all cost and no (or very, very low) benefit. But the low probability that an election will be decided by one vote also means that casting a vote has much in common with cocktail party chatter, an enjoyable activity made even more enjoyable because it can be done with impunity – it is almost completely lacking in instrumental impact. Just as people enjoy voicing support for noble objectives at cocktail parties, they enjoy doing so at the ballot box.

While Brennan and Lomasky get much of the credit for developing the concept of expressive voting and tracing out a wide range of its implications for democratic (and more generally, collective) decision making, they did have two important predecessors. Brennan and Lomasky did not find the entire $20 on the sidewalk. Based on our reading, Buchanan (1954) first picked it up, got it changed into a $10 bill, a $5 bill and five $1s, kept $1 and put the rest back on the sidewalk. Seventeen years later Tullock (1971) came along, noticed the $19 and pocketed the remaining four $1 bills. It took another 22 years before Brennan and Lomasky grabbed the remaining $15.[1]

The logic underlying expressive voting is that the opportunity cost of voting for the less beneficial option is not the value of the most beneficial option, but it is far less because of the low probability that the person voting will get the option he votes for because he voted for it. Buchanan (1954, p. 337) expressed the first awareness that voting lowers the opportunity cost of 'choosing' one option over another when he stated,

> It seems quite possible that in many instances the apparent placing of 'the public interest' above mere individual or group interest in political decisions represents nothing more than the failure of the voters to consider fully the real costs of the activity to be undertaken. It is extremely difficult to determine whether the affirmative vote of a nonbeneficiary individual for a public welfare project implies that he is either acting socially in accordance with a 'nobler' ordering of alternatives or is estimating his own self-interest in accordance with a 'collective-action' preference scale, or whether it suggests that he has failed to weigh adequately the opportunity costs of the project.

Buchanan does not explain here the failure of an individual to consider fully the value of the option not voted for in terms of the low probability that a vote will be decisive. But a few pages later (p. 339) he points out that 'the individual . . . is never secure in his belief that his vote will count positively. He may lose his vote and be placed in a position of having cast his vote in opposition to the alternative finally chosen by the social group.'

Tullock (1971) explicitly connects the low opportunity costs of voting for one option to the low probability that any vote will be decisive by considering the popularity of using government to help the poor. After contrasting the standard arguments for government transfers to the poor to the small amount actually transferred, Tullock offers his own explanation for the popularity of government charity: self interest conflicts with most people's feeling that they should help the poor, with the resulting cognitive dissonance most pronounced among intellectuals. The desire to reduce this dissonance can be satisfied at little personal cost by convincing oneself that government charity is preferable to private charity and then voting for government charity rather than actually making a charitable contribution.

But why does this 'expressive voting' (a term that Tullock did not use) not result in more money being transferred to the poor than actually is? Tullock's explanation is that people do not typically vote directly for transfer programs, but for political candidates with positions on many issues and that only those anxious to reduce the above-mentioned cognitive dissonance (a relatively few academics) will vote primarily on the basis of a politician's position on transfers to the poor.

We offer an alternative explanation for the meager amount transferred to the poor by government despite electoral support for such transfers by arguing that expressive voting seldom results in achieving the results favored by such voting. Our argument is based on an insight that Brennan and Lomasky mention briefly but do not develop, even though it allows the logic of expressive voting to enrich our understanding of democratic processes by extending it beyond the ballot box. We argue that interest group encouragement of expressive voting is the first step in victimizing members of the general public. In effect, voters are enlisted as political allies of those who exploit their gullibility. However we conclude on an optimistic note by considering the possibility that expressive voting can provide voters with their best hope for imposing discipline on their political agents.

VOTING AGAINST ONE'S INTEREST

Expressive voting is most interesting when the proposal being considered would harm (benefit) the voter, but she feels it is in (against) the public interest. People are commonly observed voting for proposals or for political candidates who favor those proposals that are against their personal interest because they feel it is in the public interest to do so. Steven Kelman (1987), like Brennan and Lomasky (1993), cites many examples of the inability to explain voting behavior and outcomes on the basis of voter self interest. Before the implications of expressive voting were developed and popularized (at least among public choice scholars) by Brennan and Lomasky, that people often, and knowingly, vote against their self interest was difficult to reconcile with the public choice view that self interest is the dominant motivation in political as well as market decisions. And if voters are more likely to consider the public interest in the political arena than they are in the marketplace, it may seem reasonable to advocate expanding the range of decisions made by government or to resist efforts to privatize, deregulate and otherwise substitute market incentives for public sector allocation.

We do not deny that people are more likely to consider the public interest when voting than when buying a pair of socks or investing in the stock market. Before concluding that this is a reason for relying more on political decisions, we should ask why voters are more public spirited than buyers/investors in the marketplace. Kelman (1987, p. 22), who clearly opposes any general reduction in the role of government, argues that 'our political institutions work to encourage public spirit. There is the elementary fact that political decisions apply to the entire community. That they do encourage people to think about others when taking a stand.' On the same page, he continues: 'Claims must become formulated in terms of general ethical arguments about rights, justice, or the public interest, . . . to stand any chance of being convincing to others.'

We have no problem with these arguments, as far as they go. First they are consistent with a fundamental proposition of public choice, that institutions matter. People do act differently when making political rather than market decisions because the rules (incentives) are different. And the public choice emphasis on self interest is not inconsistent with the recognition that the range of human motivations extends beyond narrow self interest. Indeed, Brennan and Hamlin (2000) have examined the interplay of political institutions and human motivations assuming that people are capable of other regarding behavior as well as self interested behavior.

But acknowledging that democratic political institutions elevate the importance of public interest in voting decisions is not the same as concluding that this is a good thing or that increasing our reliance on political decisions would be in the public interest. The logic of expressive voting provides a far less convoluted explanation for the importance of public interest considerations in political decisions (at least those exercised at the ballot box) than discussion of the type Kelman and others put forth. It provides a straightforward explanation for public spirited voting that is just as powerful whether we assume voters are almost entirely self interested or that they are almost entirely altruistic. Furthermore the logic of expressive voting extends easily to very unfortunate political choices made after the voting has occurred, thereby providing a far richer, but less encouraging, explanation of political outcomes than is possible by focusing exclusively on voter behavior.

The generalized logic of expressive voting is that the importance one assigns to public interest considerations is inversely related to the probability that his/her choice will determine the outcome; that is public interest considerations are more important the less responsibility the decision makers feel for the outcome of their choices (think back to Tullock's voter who votes with impunity for helping the poor because his vote will unlikely cost him anything). We see a serious downside arising from the negative connection between responsibility for outcomes and the tendency to vote for seemingly worthy social objectives.

We recognize that expressive voting can motivate election outcomes that are more efficient than would have been the case with instrumental voting (which is motivated almost entirely by self interest). Indeed one way that expressive voting could advance the public interest is, we believe, so interesting and has so much potential for good that we will consider it in some detail later in this chapter. However it will not appeal to those who see, or at least hope, that empowered government and noble intentions are forces for good. But before considering the possible social benefit from expressive voting, we must discuss the lack of responsibility at the heart of that voting which we believe is more likely to be socially harmful than beneficial. Expressive voting does often motivate people to vote against their self interests. Unfortunately, it often motivates them to vote against the interest of most other citizens as well.

VOTING AND PRISONERS' DILEMMAS

When one considers expressive voting, the first problem that comes to mind is the possibility that it puts voters in a prisoners' dilemma. Brennan and Lomasky (1993, pp. 27–8) call attention to this possibility, in which voters can be (p. 27) 'led [as if by an invisible backhand, one might say] to vote for an electoral outcome that none wants'. While we use this possibility in developing concerns about the consequences of expressive voting, the biggest problem we see arising from this voting is its exacerbation of another prisoners' dilemma found in political decision making – the one so concisely expressed by Bastiat (1995, p. 144) in his comment: 'The state is the great fictitious entity by which everyone seeks to live at the expense of everyone else.'

But before discussing some of the prisoners' dilemma implications of expressive voting, we must point out that voting, whether expressive or instrumental, also helps reduce some prisoners' dilemmas, though it always creates others. When a project that will provide collective benefits is being considered, for example, a prisoners' dilemma can easily arise if voluntary contributions are relied upon (1) to acquire information on how much the project is worth and (2) to finance it. Each individual will correctly see advantage in understating and contributing less (preferably nothing) than his anticipated benefit because of a combination of fear and hope – fear that others will free ride on his contribution and hope that he can free ride on the contribution of others. Having the decision on the project decided by voting and financed by government, if it passes, greatly reduces this prisoners' dilemma. No one has to worry about others free riding on his positive vote since no one pays unless the vote reaches the necessary threshold, in which case everyone has to pay. For the same reason, no one can hope to free ride on the contributions of others by voting against a project. But while voting moderates some prisoners' dilemmas, it creates others, the hope being that the benefit from the former is greater than the harm from the latter.

For example, citizens are collectively better off if all are well informed on the issues and political candidates in the election. Just as used car dealers provide better cars at lower prices when their customers are well informed, politicians would provide better government programs at lower cost if voters were better informed. The costs to becoming informed are much the same with information on market and political decisions, but the benefits are not. In the marketplace, the quality of the decision a person makes and the benefit he receives are tightly connected, whereas each voter knows that his decision will have almost no effect on the government services he receives or how much he pays for them, no matter how informed his vote. This is true no matter what he thinks other voters will do, unless he assumes unrealistically that other voters will split their votes evenly, in which case his vote is decisive. So for each citizen it is rational to remain politically uninformed (numerous surveys show that most people are woefully uninformed on candidates and issues) even though the resulting 'rational ignorance' leads to worse outcomes for citizens in general. This prisoners' dilemma is known as 'rational ignorance.'

Even if information were free and citizens were fully informed, they would still be in a voting prisoners' dilemma. Those who take the time to register and vote incur personal costs. These costs are not large, but larger than any benefit a voter realizes from shifting political decisions in the direction she prefers. So though it may be collectively rational for all informed voters to vote, since this would keep politicians more responsive to the general concerns of the public, voting is irrational (at least for the purpose of affecting the outcome) from the perspective of each voter. This prisoners' dilemma is commonly referred to as 'rational apathy.'

It is not clear how these prisoners' dilemmas can be overcome, and for many decisions their harm is surely less than the benefits voting provides by moderating other prisoners' dilemmas associated with collective decision making. But acknowledging that prisoners' dilemmas are inherent in voting is important if we are to recognize that voting can do more harm than good unless it is restricted to making decisions where the case for making them collectively is compelling.

EXPRESSIVE VOTING AND PRISONERS' DILEMMAS: CAUSE OR CURE?

That rational voter apathy is a serious prisoners' dilemma can be criticized by pointing out that many, and often most, eligible voters do go to the polls and vote. The level of voter participation indicates rather strongly that people must realize personal benefits from voting that are not captured by the instrumental effects or their votes. The value people place on the expressive aspects of voting is a powerful explanation for the observed level of voter participation, but this explanation simply shifts the focus from one prisoners' dilemma to another. The expressive benefits that reduce the prisoners' dilemma of rational apathy entangle voters in another one. As Brennan and Lomasky point out, expressive voting can put voters in a prisoners' dilemma in which the cost of each voter's expression is spread out over all other voters as an externality of the type embedded in all prisoners' dilemmas.

We acknowledge at this point that although externalities are embedded in all prisoners' dilemmas, it does not follow that the externality associated with expressive voting necessarily leads to a prisoners' dilemma. An externality is associated with all voting, expressive or otherwise, but it can serve to remove voters from a prisoners' dilemma as previously indicated. All voting involves making choices that impact the welfare of others, but these external impacts can be either positive or negative. For example, each person's vote in favor of pollution control, even if motivated entirely by instrumental considerations, creates a positive externality when everyone is suffering more from the pollution of others than benefiting from their own. Of course, reducing pollution is the type of issue likely to motivate expressive voting, with people possibly voting for pollution control that costs them more than the benefit they receive. So while negative externalities from expressive voting can result in a vote for too much pollution control, this is not always the case.

Consider a situation in which pollution does not harm all polluters – some may be benefiting from polluting others – with the majority of the voters receiving small benefits from pollution that imposes large costs on the minority. In this case if voting is motivated solely by instrumental concerns, the efficient level of pollution control will be voted down. But if people vote on the basis of expressive concerns, and they likely will, then many who would be personally harmed by the enforcement of the efficient level of pollution will vote for it anyway, and the proposal to reduce pollution to that level will pass. So expressive voting can result in an efficient vote by generating positive voting externalities in situations where instrumental voting would have resulted in an inefficient vote by generating negative externalities.

But when the effects of political decision making are extended beyond the voting booth, the efficiency implications of expressive voting become more dubious. In the preceding paragraph, we simply assumed that somehow the efficient level of pollution, along with the best type of pollution control and degree of enforcement, had been determined.[2] But these decisions are not made by voters but by politicians, government officials and organized groups in response to competing public and private interests subject to political constraints, including those imposed by the decisions of voters. And expressive voting does more to ease (or less to tighten) the constraints voters impose on government than does instrumental voting when the issue involves increasing government power to do things perceived as virtuous.

Once voters authorize government to take more of their money and exercise more power for some worthy purpose, they find themselves in another prisoners' dilemma. Even if the objective voted for would be efficient, as well as worthy, if pursued with the dedication and cost effectiveness that voters desire and have been led to expect, achieving this efficiency requires that voters follow up their votes by monitoring their political agents. But monitoring the actual result of expanded political power is far more costly than casting a virtuous vote, and most expressive voters are content with the temporary feeling of righteousness provided by their vote. The demand curve for feeling righteous is downward sloping like the demand curve for popcorn, and surely more elastic.

So even if expressive voting allows voters to escape one prisoners' dilemma, it throws them into another. Voters would be collectively better off if all contributed to the cost of monitoring how the power their expressive votes give to political authorities is used, but each taxpayer is better off not contributing, no matter what she thinks others will do. So once voters have approved a government program to accomplish some worthy social goal, organized groups working behind the scenes can design and implement the program so that it does more to promote their interests than achieve the worthy goal.

Of course, members of politically organized groups have the same desire to promote laudable social objectives as anyone else. But expect them to behave with less regard for those objectives in their roles as members of organized interest groups than as expressive voters because of a difference in incentives – a difference that follows immediately from the logic of expressive voting. Because most interest groups are relatively small with each having a dominant interest, they can organize and take effective political action more easily than voters. So unlike voters, an organized group will very likely have a decisive impact on political outcomes very important to its members. Members of interest groups may have the same demand for virtue as voters in general, but the cost of casting their 'vote' (political influence) in favor of noble social objectives is far higher in terms of the private benefits sacrificed.[3] And it is not just the cost side operating here. There is a very good and extremely popular substitute for achieving a feeling of virtue by sacrificing private advantage: achieving a feeling of virtue without the sacrifice. Few things are easier than convincing ourselves that the policies that benefit us the most will also benefit society the most. So do not expect special interests to use their political influence to favor policies that threaten their private interest.

Unfortunately what is good for interest groups is not always good for the general public, and political actions designed to favor particular interest groups quite often victimize the general public. But it takes more than just special interest influence to move legislation through the political process, particularly legislation harmful to the public. Public opinion is important to the success of legislation, since it is almost impossible to enact a policy in the face of strong public hostility, no matter how much an organized interest favors it. Interest groups must convince a significant segment of the public that their special interest proposals are either directly beneficial to voters or deserve their support on grounds of social justice. Unfortunately, organized interests often have little trouble convincing the public to vote for proposals that destroy wealth and lack redeeming social merit. The rational ignorance of most voters makes them gullible to plausible sounding but fraudulent claims about policies that end up harming them and the causes they support. Expressive voting and rational ignorance are easily exploited by interest groups who benefit from those policies to enlist voters as allies in support of their own victimization.

Victimization is not too strong a word for what often happens to voters when they vote to expand government to pursue noble objectives. Examples are numerous of interest groups using noble objectives to manipulate voter approval of economically destructive programs that allow them to capture transfers from the general public. Voters want to protect American jobs and are easily convinced that tariffs and import restrictions are the best way of doing so; voters want to save the family farm and are easily convinced that this requires agricultural price supports and subsidies; voters want to help the poor and are easily convinced that poor people benefit from minimum wages and rent controls; voters want good educational opportunities for children and are easily convinced that the same desire motivates opposition to school vouchers by public school unions; voters want to protect American consumers against unqualified workers and are easily convinced that this is the purpose of occupational licensing; voters want to prevent large corporations from endangering their customers with inferior products and are easily convinced that this is the effect of legislation facilitating class action lawsuits and so on. Even if under certain circumstances a case can be made for some of the above policies on public interest grounds, it is doubtful that any informed person would approve of the effects of these policies that end up designed and implemented under the influence of politically active interest groups.

Brennan and Lomasky recognize that expressive voting is just the first stage in a two stage political process, with organized interests exerting more influence on the details of achieving the broad objectives desired by expressive voters. For example, they state (1993, p. 88),

> When it comes to the *detail* of particular policies, interests are more likely to emerge as relevant and this for two reasons: first, because lobbying activity as well as voting is relevant to the determination of policy, and lobbying is often more relevant to the details of policy; second, because expressive returns are generally a matter of the overall symbolic aura of policy and not details of execution. (emphasis in original)

We obviously agree with this statement as far as it goes, but we do not think Brennan and Lomasky take their analysis far enough. As just discussed, we see voters' lack of control over the details of policy compared to the control interest groups exert as a direct implication of expressive voting, and one that suggests a serious problem with the consequences of that voting, a consequence that Brennan and Lomasky seem to ignore. Nowhere in their book do we find any indication that the logic of expressive voting implies interest groups will influence the details of policies so they have effects quite the opposite of those which voters feel good about supporting. People may be willing to cast low cost votes for worthy goals that would impose some personal sacrifice on them, but we doubt they would do so to allow a privileged few to subvert those goals to pad their pockets at public expense. We believe this is exactly what expressive and rationally ignorant voters often do. We also believe it offers a better explanation than the one Tullock (1971) offers (which we discussed in the first section of this chapter) for his observation that far less money is transferred to the poor by government programs than is voted for.

By extending the logic of expressive voting farther than Brennan and Lomasky do, applying it to the choices of interest groups as well as to the choices of voters, we reach a more pessimistic conclusion on expressive voting than they do. As explained earlier, organized interests do not cast their 'votes' (influence) expressively for noble goals, because as opposed to those regular voters, the 'votes' of organized interests significantly affect political outcomes. The payoff to interest groups is not in realizing fleeting feelings of virtue by voting for noble pursuits but in sabotaging those pursuits for more substantive advantage. The point is not that expressive voters are more moral than members of interest groups but that the private cost of voting for noble goals is far less than using effective influence to actually achieve those goals.

But interest groups should not see their political influence as an unblemished blessing. That interest groups can gain private benefits at public expense puts them into yet another prisoners' dilemma. If there were only a few politically influential interest groups, then there would be no serious prisoners' dilemma from their perspective. Piracy is profitable when the pirates are few and the victims are many. But profits attract imitators, and more and more politically motivated interest groups will form once people see the advantage in exercising political influence for private gain. Of course, when almost everyone becomes a pirate and less effort goes into shipping the goods, everyone becomes worse off. And today almost everyone is a member of one interest group or another benefiting from some government program that harms the general public. We obviously have not reached the point where there is no payoff to shipping the goods, but the payoff is less than it would be without the existing level of special interest politics. But there is little incentive for anyone to start reversing the trend by redirecting effort and resources out of political predation and back into productive activity even though we would all be better off if everyone did. Who wants to lower his Jolly Roger and devote himself entirely to shipping the goods when he is surrounded by pirates?

Expressive voting can lead to a prisoners' dilemma, as shown by Brennan and Lomasky (1993, pp. 27–8). But expressive voting can be seen as either socially harmful or helpful when only the first stage of the political process is considered – as noted above, it can be the means of overcoming prisoners' dilemmas as well as the cause of them. Only by considering the second stage of the political process, where the power expressive voters grant government to pursue noble goals is captured by interest groups for nefarious purposes, do we get a more complete and less optimistic perspective on the social benefit of expressive voting.

Our analysis of expressive voting is not entirely devoid of optimism, however. We now consider an implication of expressive voting that may hold more appeal to us than it will to those who see social promise in the support of noble sentiments by expressive voters.

CONSTRUCTIVE SKEPTICISM OR DESTRUCTIVE CYNICISM?

The most serious problem we see with expressive voting is that it can convert noble sentiments into opportunities for interest groups to capture private benefits with socially destructive policies with everyone being harmed, even members of the interest groups. But by the logic of expressive voting, voting behavior at the individual level is extremely sensitive to what one sees as noble which is in the eye of the beholder. This follows immediately from the formulation of the central result of expressive voting presented by Brennan and Lomasky as inequality (2.7) on p. 27,

$$L_A - L_B > h(R_B - R_A)^4$$

where L_A is the expressive value the voter realizes from voting for option A, L_B is the expressive value she realizes from voting for option B, R_A is the instrumental value she realizes if option A passes, R_B is the instrumental value she realizes if option B passes, and h is the probability that her vote will be decisive. Obviously, if this inequality holds, the voter realizes the greatest personal benefit by voting for A instead of B.

The interesting case is when $L_A - L_B$ is positive, but less than $R_B - R_A$ (the instrumental value of B passing instead of A is greater than the positive expressive value of voting for A instead of B). Because h is almost sure to have a value extremely close to zero, even if $R_B - R_A$ is much larger than $L_A - L_B$, the largest payoff will likely be in voting for A. Expressive payoffs will, of course, be quite small for most voters. Few would be willing to sacrifice more than the price of a soft drink for that fleeting glow of virtue from voting with their hearts rather than their pocketbooks. But of course, even a very small expressive payoff is a bargain given its very low cost in terms of instrumental sacrifice. For example, even if $R_B - R_A$ is equal to $5000 to an individual, if the probability of his vote being decisive is 1/20 000, then the expected cost of voting for A is only 25 cents, and 1/20 000 is an unrealistically high probability of a decisive vote in almost any election in which a typical voter has $5000 at stake on the outcome.[5] So if the voter's $L_A - L_B$ is just $0.50, he gets a bargain in expressive satisfaction by voting against his material wellbeing.

But this means that a small reduction in the value voters place on expressing support for the superficially noble could have a large impact on voting outcomes. We see this as the optimistic side of expressive voting. If somehow voters, or at least a significant number of them, are convinced that there is no virtue in voting for most political proposals or the politicians who support them, no matter how virtuous those proposals are claimed to be, then expressive voting will no longer create political power that will be captured and contaminated by organized interests. Or voters could be convinced that the real virtue is in passing up the cheap sense of virtue from voting for feelgood proposals and voting against such proposals.

Convincing people of the virtue of voting against noble sounding proposals may be difficult, but it is certainly possible. This possibility, along with the logic of expressive voting, provides hope for constraining government that is hard to find in the standard public choice story of powerful organized interests exploiting rationally ignorant and apathetic voters through a proliferation of special interest government programs. Once the importance of expressive motivations in voting is recognized, voter apathy is no longer rational, and understandings about the dangers of special interest politics that for a long time dominated public opinion in the Western democracies, especially in the United States, can mobilize voters to reverse government growth and undermine the power of organized interests.[6]

We recognize that what we see as empowering voters with a constructive skepticism toward government attempts to pursue noble purposes will be seen by some as destructive cynicism. Certainly, like everything else, our constructive skepticism comes at a cost. Some government actions (or expansions) that would be socially desirable, even with interest group manipulation, would be blocked (or scaled down) by our skeptical expressive voters. But we believe that this cost would be more than offset by the socially harmful proposals that would be stillborn or never conceived in the first place. Indeed, eliminating many of the harmful proposals could easily result in achieving more of the desirable objectives because of the additional wealth created by reducing the resources wasted in what Bastiat described as everyone's seeking to live at the expense of everyone else. It is difficult to think of desirable objectives that are not more effectively addressed in richer economies than poorer ones. Even objectives that many people believe government action can pursue in ways that create net social benefits – such as poverty reduction, better education, a cleaner environmental and improved medical care – will be achieved to a greater degree in the long run because of the additional wealth generated when political proposals face skeptical voters rather than trusting voters.

But is not there a danger that encouraging a negative attitude toward noble pursuits by government will lead toward a callous disregard of such pursuits in general or worse? Most of Brennan and Lomasky's discussion focuses on the expression of admirable objectives at the polls, but they recognize that benevolence is only one side of the spectrum of human sentiments. Malicious attitudes can be a serious problem when expressed at the polls, since, as Brennan and Lomasky point out on page 174: 'Expressions of malice and/or envy no less than expressions of altruism are cheaper in the voting booth than in the market.' But we are not convinced that those who like to think of themselves as motivated by the loftiest of sentiments and vote in the belief that these sentiments are best carried out by government, are any less capable of yielding to malevolent impulses than are those who distrust government's ability to convert noble sentiments into noble outcomes.

Furthermore, we think that the case for encouraging a skeptical view of government virtue is strengthened by the malevolent feelings that are seldom far beneath the surface and which can easily erupt in response to frustrations and aggravations. Our best safeguard against the abuse of government power created by the expressive urges of voters, both when they are trusting and when they are skeptical of government, is constitutional limits on what government can do regardless of majority sentiment. But such constitutional limits and their effectiveness depend on supporting public opinion. In the words of Henry Simons (1951, p. 20): 'Constitutional provisions are no stronger than the consensus that they articulate.' Or, as stated by Brennan and Lomasky (p. 223): 'Expressive considerations will themselves intrude every bit as much at the constitutional level of collective choice as at the in period level.' Our perspective is that strict constitutional limits on government are necessary to protect us against political power that is too responsive to expressive voting, and public skepticism regarding the benefits of political power is useful, and probably necessary, if we are to impose those strict constitutional limits.

Increasing the scope and power of government increases the potential that expressing our frustrations and animosities through voting will be transformed into action that imposes harm, and likely atrocities, on the most vulnerable members of society. Before dismissing this comment as extreme, consider the politically inspired horrors of the twentieth century. Professor R.J. Rummel (1994) of the University of Hawaii at Manoa estimates that there were approximately 37 million battlefield deaths from 1900 to around 1990. And this is only the start. Rummel also estimates that over the same period, governments massacred or willfully starved approximately 150 million noncombatants (mostly their own citizens). Granted, most of this carnage was the result of non-democratic governments, but not all. And we do not think it is extreme to argue that all governments, including democratic ones, are safer governments when the public is skeptical of the good that can be accomplished with government power.

CONCLUSION

While we are not sure that Brennan and Lomasky will agree with all or even much of our chapter, we are sure that they are its intellectual parents. As with biological procreation, intellectual procreation is risky business, and neither type of parent has any guarantee that they will be proud of their offspring. We recognize that disappointment can be more the fault of clumsy midwives than of the parents, and as the midwives to this chapter, we are quite willing to accept a large measure of the blame for any disappointment with which it is received.

But that is not to say that we are not pleased or even proud of the result. In writing *Democracy and Decision: The Pure Theory of Electoral Preference*, Brennan and Lomasky took the straightforward idea of expressive voting and blended it with an impressive knowledge of political philosophy and public choice to develop insights with rich and far reaching implications for issues of enduring interest and importance. As with all truly creative scholarship, there is no way of anticipating fully where the implications of expressive voting will lead. We feel that we have followed one of those implications down an interesting path, though one that not all will find completely comforting, and no doubt some will believe that the logic of our argument wandered off the path and got lost in the underbrush. But regardless of the fate of this chapter, it has impressive parentage and will have a host of productive siblings.

NOTES

1. One can argue over the relative contributions of Buchanan, Tullock, and Brennan and Lomasky. Possibly Buchanan deserves credit for more than 1/20 of the contribution by being the first (that we are aware of) to identify what Brennan and Lomasky later termed expressive voting. But as we shall see, he mentions this logic only briefly, although it is worth pointing out that his insight predates Downs' development of rational apathy and ignorance by three years. We credit Tullock for 4/20 of the contribution because he built his entire paper around the logic of expressive voting.

2. The efficient level of pollution obviously depends on the type of enforcement. In general, the less costly the control, the less the efficient level of pollution.

3. The logic here is stated by Brennan and Lomasky (1993, p. 26) when they point out, 'If we imagine a spectrum running from the case in which the chooser is decisive through cases in which the chances of his being decisive are increasingly remote, then the role of expressive rather than instrumental elements in preference revelation increases along that spectrum until, in the limit, expressive considerations become the sole determinant of 'choice behavior.' Although Brennan and Lomasky recognize that interest groups are more interested in the details of policy than voters (as shown below), they do not explain this difference in terms of the logic in the above statement.

4. In their book, Brennan and Lomasky mistakenly reverse the order of R_A and R_B on the right-hand side of the inequality.

5. See Chapter 4 of Brennan and Lomasky for a mathematical development of the probabilities of electoral decisiveness. Unless the probability is 0.5 that each voter will vote for A, and the same for B, the probability of a tied election quickly becomes arbitrarily close to zero as the number of voters increases to numbers far less than vote in state and federal elections.

6. Based on our own experience, conversations with friends and casual observations, we believe that many people currently vote expressively against government expenditures, even in cases where they would realize private benefits from those expenditures. We have both voted against spending at the state level that would, and in some cases did, benefit us personally, and which we would probably have voted for if we had thought our votes would be decisive. Surely, given the percentage of the voting-age population that works

for government and the percentage who votes Republican (admittedly not a great proxy for voting against government spending), there is clearly enough overlap to find many people whose financial interest is positively related to government expenditures that they express opposition to in their voting.

REFERENCES

Bastiat, Frederic (1995), *Selected Essays on Political Economy*, Irvington-on-Hudson, US: The Foundation for Economic Education.

Brennan, Geoffrey and Loren Lomasky (1993), *Democracy and Decision: The Pure Theory of Electoral Preference*, New York: Cambridge University Press.

Brennan, Geoffrey and Alan Hamlin (2000), *Democratic Devices and Desires*, Cambridge: Cambridge University Press.

Buchanan, James M. (1954), 'Individual Choice in Voting and the Market', *The Journal of Political Economy*, **62** (4), 334–43.

Downs, Anthony (1957), *An Economic Theory of Democracy*, New York: Harper & Row.

Kelman, Steven (1987), *Making Public Policy: A Hopeful View of American Government*, New York: Basic Books, Inc.

Rummel, R.J. (1994), *Death by Government: Genocide and Mass Murder in the Twentieth Century*, New Brunswick, US: Transaction Publishers.

Simons, Henry C. (1951), *Economic Policy for a Free Society*, Chicago: University of Chicago Press.

Tullock, Gordon (1971), 'The Charity of the Uncharitable', *Western Economic Journal*, **9**, 379–92.

3. Who shall keep the keepers themselves? On the moral foundations of the separation of powers

Giuseppe Eusepi

If 'market failure' was to be diagnosed on the basis of market agents acting in an entirely self-interested fashion, it would seem hopelessly biased ideologically to proclaim 'political success' on the basis of agents acting in an exclusively benevolent fashion.
. . . there does not seem to be any a priori reason
why this third player [the Constitutional Court]
would reliably enforce contracts between the other two. (Geoffrey Brennan, 2000, 'Trust adjudication and the *quis custodiet* problem')

INTRODUCTION

It is obvious that, in an anarchic setting where there are no rules, there does not exist a problem of who shall keep the keeper himself. The situation is less obvious where a body of rules exists, but power is undivided. In the latter setting, rules are not independent of the keeper, for they are the very expression of his exclusive will.

In spite of the fact that Anglo-Saxons often refer to Hobbes's *Leviathan* in discussing such a situation, the *Prince* envisaged by Machiavelli is much more akin to the case of the benevolent despot because Hobbes's contract lacks the basic presupposition on which a contract hinges: moral equality between the contracting parties. Hobbes's contract would be coherent only if each individual had agreed without fear, or constraint, by an act of unlimited trust, that he should be governed by a sovereign with absolute power. If one would seek to illuminate this kind of setting, one should assume that subjects are translucent because only under this condition could the sovereign measure his subjects' level of trustworthiness. But if a sovereign were able to do so, he would have no reason to contrast the separation of powers, which is incompatible with *ad hoc* morals. It is precisely for this reason that

Machiavelli offers greater insight than Hobbes, for Machiavelli explicitly endows his world with two morals – one for the Prince himself and another for his subjects. In such a context, the Prince's keeper – provided that such an expression makes sense at all – could be no-one but the Prince himself. The consequence is that a rule will be either respected or changed according to the Prince's self-interest.

These, however, are only speculative notions. The reason I do not want to indulge further on this line of enquiry is that this does not reflect the political–institutional setting where my reasoning originates. Instead, I turn to a setting where powers are separated to give an account of if and how the delegation of power actually works. In the context of my investigation, it is interesting to analyse the behaviour of the judges of the constitutional court when the government is one of the conflicting parties. To see whether judges are reliable keepers of the constitution or not, I shall use what I define, in an attempt to label Brennan's scrutiny of the problem, the *compound symmetry paradigm*. I shall try to demystify the role of constitutional courts in Western democracies and provide a reply to the often-asked question: Is the constitutional court, which has been empowered to keep the keepers, an impartial institution that prevents dictatorial solutions? Or is it rather a pro-government institution that ends up by giving a legal gloss to majoritarian tyranny? To answer these questions I shall focus on the Italian Constitutional Court. In particular, attention will be given to the possible devices that can be introduced to limit rent-seeking activities by the government and to the measures to be put in place to prevent judges from behaving as informal agents of the government. It is, in fact, implausible that an additional judge be appointed with the aim of watching the behaviour of the judges of the constitutional court without falling, for the sake of perfection, into a sort of infinite regress.

THE NO-POWER/ALL-POWER ALTERNATIVE

To start a work, whose aim is to extend Brennan's contribution to the understanding of the classical problem of 'who shall keep the keepers themselves', with a section dealing with the anarchy/absolutism paradigm might expose the author to the same critique addressed to one who sets out to write a history of the motor-car by beginning with a dissertation on the evolution of the ox-cart. However, it was not the impulse of completeness that moved me to write this section. It was rather my eagerness to see the moral implications embodied in the passage from anarchy to absolutism, since moral implications are of cardinal importance in any consideration regarding the separation of powers.

If men were angels, anarchy would be the best of the possible worlds. This vision recalls the Rousseauian world of anarchy where individuals were natural and uncorrupted. This state of happy anarchy, however, comes to an end with the establishment of property, science and arts that are responsible for the corruption of men. Such a vision finds no audience among Public Choice scholars since, in a world free from scarcity and related conflicts, there is no reason for rules. The Rousseauian anarchy describes a perfect and ideal world. Yet though this would be the only world able to work in the absence of either rules or power, it cannot be realised because men are not angels. The anarchic original setting, whether it be Hobbesian or Lockeian, is characterised by scarcity, so conflicts among individuals are unavoidable and cannot be solved peacefully due to the absence of rules. The survival threshold of the individual then critically depends on the force with which he defends his own body, the products of his work, or his ability to take possession of his fellow men's products.

In a context of this sort, according to Hobbes, the rejection of war and the objective of peace would induce individuals to subdue to the Leviathan with what I define a quasi-universal decision, it being the individual destined to become Leviathan the only one who rests in the state of nature. This is what the Hobbesian social contract is all about. Through this social contract there is a shift from anarchy to absolute power where double morals – one for the Leviathan; another for his subjects – is a convenient umbrella for giving moral coverage to the Leviathan's act of enslaving his subjects.

However different from anarchy absolute power might be, it still has an element in common with it for there is no possibility, not even conceptual, of controlling the keeper, which in the case of absolute power not only exists, but has no limits at all. Clearly, neither anarchy nor absolutism leave any room for the keeper's keeper, but in absolutism the subjects' moral position is far worse. Paraphrasing Buchanan's words, what individuals lose in the passage from anarchy to Leviathan is a sort of moral equality. This point needs to be clarified. I do not want to maintain that anarchy is morally preferable, in a general sense, to Leviathan. I am assuming, following in the footsteps of Buchanan, that anarchy also entails moral anarchy, that is the absence of morals in a genuine sense.

My conjecture is simply an attempt to explain the origin of morals in an absolute setting as stemming from a discriminatory act. This implication invites one serious problem. Paradoxically, a morally discriminatory act turns out to be the foundation of morals themselves. All this could find no place in the Kantian framework of the categorical imperative, or in the dicta as recognised by the present-age common sense.

Since for Hobbes the alternative to perennial disorder is undivided power, which requires an absolute order, there is no way to make that order consensual, for the very existence of moral discrimination. Despite Hobbes's interpretation, *homo economicus* can be thought of as the element that has the greatest impact in the passage from anarchy to Leviathan.

While in anarchy all individuals have the potential to be *homines economici*, in an absolutist setting the Leviathan would be the only *homo economicus*. This is an indirect way of showing that the shift from anarchy to Leviathan cannot be explained by reference to a contract. If this were the case, it would not be hard to imagine that rational *homines economici* might be induced to prefer anarchy to Leviathan. Such a choice carries with it that each subject, save the Leviathan, waives any right to pursue his own interest, so becoming a purely altruistic individual. If one modifies, even very marginally, the paradigm of purely altruistic men and, adding a little realism, admit that some of those men are driven by incentives that are not fully altruistic and few, very few (theoretically one person only) are driven by pure egoism, altruists will be inexorably eliminated. Still more, if pure altruists inhabited an absolutist world, there would be no reason for them to exit from absolutism.

In *The Prince*, Machiavelli makes the point well: 'For a man who, in all respects, will carry out only his professions of good, will be apt to be ruined amongst so many who are evil'.[1] If, then, man is rational, the economic man is not such at all. This is the reason why he decides to leap out of anarchy – where he was able, although in a very special sense, to pursue his own interests – to commit himself *in toto* to the Leviathan. Genuine rational men would give up the use of force only on condition that the alternative were not that of assigning rule-making power to the Leviathan. The genuine rational man takes into account the reciprocity principle and accordingly would willingly give up the use of force in favour of consensual rules as opposed to the Leviathan.

All this, however, seems to run counter to Buchanan's conclusions that have shaped and influenced so large a part of scholarship in this field. His way of overcoming chaos by means of the Hobbesian contract seems to involve systematic moral discrimination. In a sense, paraphrasing Buchanan himself, one could say that the exit from economic chaos gives rise to moral chaos or, better, moral discrimination. It is over moral discrimination that Hobbes is silent, while Machiavelli, who fully catches its importance, justifies moral discrimination as the inevitable cost to create and maintain his Prince. Further, Machiavelli does not resort to the expedient of the contract to justify absolutism. In fact, he takes absolutism as a point of departure, or initial status quo, and simply illustrates the essential elements necessary to his Prince. For Machiavelli the Prince has to be endowed at once with the strength of the lion and the shrewdness of the fox. Strength and shrewdness exist side by side. It is this combination that gives the Prince the privilege of escaping the constraints of ordinary men's morals.[2] In his words: 'A prince should be a fox, to know the traps and snares; and a lion, to be able to frighten the wolves; for those who simply hold to the nature of the lion do not understand their business'.[3]

THE COMPOUND SYMMETRY PARADIGM

Extremist or elementary reasoning that sees the individual as either totally egoistical or totally altruistic, may be regarded as inconsistent with the separation of powers. Contrary to what may appear *prima facie*, pure altruism has a stake in scarcity although for different reasons than those underlying pure egoism's stake. If the state of nature were that depicted by classical poets and labelled as the 'golden age', or the world of men-angels, individuals would have been rationally altruist and there would have been no reason to limit altruism through the establishment of private property, nor any need for judges to sanction the violations of such property. The existence of property and judges, who restore property rights once they have been violated, is justified ultimately by scarcity. It is, in fact, scarcity that generates egoism and induces men, certainly not spurred by reason, to treat their fellow-human beings as different from themselves. Hence, the more scarcity increases, the more conflicts arise, so making the need for a judge necessary.

One could say that in the vision of the pure *homo economicus* or entirely egoistical man, there is an anti-contractual or anti-social attitude, while in the purely altruistic vision the anti-individual component is so powerful that it undermines the individual's entitlement to choose. Brennan's aversion to pure versions, which the normative theory so strictly depends on, does not arise from a politically moderate view *per se*. It rather emerges from a *methodologically appropriate* vision based on the conviction that if the individual is the Buchanan elementary decision-making unit, he can adjust to different contexts only in *marginal* and subjective terms, and not in a *total* or *objective way*. And the individual adopts such a position either when he is assumed to respond to the incentives offered by wearing 'two hats' (that is, by acting under different motivational structures in different circumstances) or when he takes fully abstract positions, as in standard Public Choice. At a first sight, a position of this sort seems to respond to an internal consistency; on a second view, however, it perverts the whole framework of the subjective theory of opportunity cost. The concept of compound symmetry canvassed here, which derives from Brennan's analysis, can be viewed as a tool to gain a greater depth of insight into the subjective theory of opportunity cost.

Since this chapter is directly provoked by reading Geoffrey Brennan's 'Trust, adjudication and the *quis custodiet* problem' (2000) the best way of answering the question of who shall keep the keepers themselves is to start with his central propositions that are the basis for presenting my concept of compound symmetry. Compound symmetry helps me to unearth Brennan's unconventional methodology that is innovative compared to the more restrictive version of methodological individualism from which standard Public Choice starts. Brennan also provides us with insights that are transferable to the political market for votes – especially useful in evaluating the weight and significance of the vote for each voter – and that go well beyond the specific subject matter analysed here.[4]

According to the concept of compound symmetry, which espouses the Smithian principle of sympathy, each individual harbours two motivational components – egoism and altruism – that influence the individual's evaluations and related decisions. Differently combined for each individual *i* α_i BENEVOLENCE + $(1 - \alpha_i)$ EGOISM with $\alpha_i \in [0,1]$, as in Figure 3.1, the cases of full egoism (*homo economicus*) and full altruism (*homo politicus*) are then simply the extreme cases of individual *compoundness* when $\alpha_i = 0$ or $\alpha_i = 1$. The compound symmetry paradigm justifies the reciprocity principle as a moral or general criterion, which involves a radical critique of extremist or polar visions.

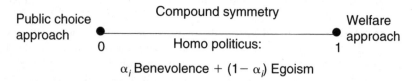

Figure 3.1   The compound symmetry line with a varying α

The individual Brennan starts from recalls standard Public Choice for the symmetry criterion only. In fact his symmetry is a particular one in that individuals are 'somewhat benevolent; somewhat publicly-interested'[5] both in the market and in voting. The comparison between egoism and altruism may prove to be apposite for an understanding of the potential conflicts between the *homo economicus* and the *homo politicus* component; the behavioural symmetry of standard Public Choice notwithstanding. Such conflicts, which could be attributed to adjustment mechanisms in both the economic and the political market, can be mitigated when approached from a slightly different angle as Brennan does. He deliberately excludes from his analysis pure egoism and pure altruism at the individual level as well as extreme or pure versions of anarchy and Leviathan at the institutional level. These two paradigms have become the battleground of standard Public

Choice and welfare economics respectively. Therefore, the critique expressed by Brennan about pure extremism is addressed to both trends of thought.[6]

Brennan points in the direction of a Kantian world, when he denies that 'the rulers are in any way morally superior to, or more benevolent, than the ruled'.[7] The behavioural symmetry of standard Public Choice originated and developed in the extreme context of the pure *homo economicus*, while the pure asymmetry of welfare economics was based on the pure or fully benevolent *homo politicus*. For Brennan all pure versions have little to do with genuine individuals who think, evaluate and choose in the real world. Purely egoistical individuals as promoted by the Neoclassicists are caricatures of real individuals. So are purely altruistic individuals. These individuals are consistent only if one accepts a one-dimensional conception of individuals whose behaviours are purely mechanical and embedded in the objective theory of cost. Exactly for these reasons the idea of compound symmetry repudiates pure forms of egoism–altruism. Compound symmetry and pure egoism–altruism are then mutually exclusive.

Brennan has contributed to freeing models of the individual from extreme, one-faceted classifications and has provided a less rigid paradigm of human behaviour. And, in fact, both standard Public Choice, which had been shaped for theoretical purposes, and welfare economics, turned out to be inapplicable to the real world. Compound symmetry moves forward to a new type of individual different from either *homo economics* or *homo politicus*. This individual is one who subsumes egoism and altruism, although in different degrees.

Compound symmetry might be regarded as limiting the choice of individuals to be launched into politics to those who are more inclined to altruism, thus excluding persons who lean towards egoism from the political arena. This possible misinterpretation notwithstanding, it is easy to show that both the pure symmetry paradigm and the pure asymmetry one are methodologically objectionable, not only in the Hobbes–Hume version, but even in the most recent versions of behavioural homogeneity *à la* Buchanan (1975) or Frey (1997), which seem to exclude *motivational heterogeneity*.[8] Since heterogeneity is inborn in compound symmetry, individual differences are in terms of margins and not totality.[9]

It is worth noting, however, that by introducing heterogeneous individuals, it is unlikely that the scenario will go a step beyond the Platonic representation where feasibility problems are intentionally omitted, and so my effort would be confined to nothing more than a typical discourse from the ivory tower. The overcoming of this Platonic abstract construction requires that a mechanism exists to select only those individuals more prone to altruism and, consequently, to exclude those more prone to self-interest. But there is not any such an electoral system able to distinguish, to use Brennan's words, 'the good guys from the bad'.[10] The reason for this is that both those individuals who are predominantly egoist and those who are predominantly altruist are interested in taking over public offices. However, altruistic and egoistic motivations are inner elements of individuals that cannot be revealed, or falsified, reliably by the individuals themselves. No device able to capture perfectly the genuine inner motivations can be thought up in the delegation process. Discerning 'the good' and 'the bad' *ex ante* is too difficult a problem for the delegation process to solve. Therefore one could think that the construction of compound symmetry is an artificial compromise that hardly explains the individuals' behaviour in the Western institutional setting. If all men were pure altruists, there would not be any justification for the division of powers or for the existence of judges. But, what matters more, altruism would be destined to remain a pure hypothesis because it could be unobservable by an impartial spectator. For altruistic behaviour to be really observable, and to result in exchanges, one should assume that there is at least a small fraction of individuals who behave egoistically.

KANTIAN CATEGORICAL IMPERATIVE OR HOBBESIANISM?

The legal order of the Western world – based on Kantian morals and on the separation of powers – requires that all powers abide by the law. This does not simply imply that there are no powers *legibus soluti*; it means also that political equality is determined by the law.

Starting from such an analysis, all emerging conflicts, as evidenced recently by Kliemt (2004), have to find their solutions in a judicial verdict. Whatever conclusion one reaches about conflicts, there can be no doubt that when conflicts deal with the assignment of competences to the various powers, only the constitutional court is entitled to deliver the final verdict. Kliemt has shown the strength of the risk that international relationships – run according to a Hobbesian logic – will jeopardise the Western constitutional system. For in international relationships there is no final verdict delivered by an international constitutional court. If my reading of Kliemt's stance is correct, he assumes that the final verdict delivered by Western constitutional courts is always expressed by judges acting as third parties. It is exactly the guarantee of being a third party *vis à vis* the powers in conflict that, according to Kliemt, sets the Western legal system on a superior level. Yet, full independence of constitutional judges, and *a fortiori* constitutional courts, cannot be taken for granted. My critique is not a matter of principle, but it is grounded on a feasibility argument and this is so even if one starts from a position of compound symmetry.

In short, while for Kliemt the threat to the Western moral–legal system can come only from the possible indirect impact of international relationships (terrorism is a very convincing current example), I identify the potential Achilles' heel of the whole structure of the separation of powers in the difficulty of establishing a judge as a genuine third party. And this difficulty increases when the government is one of the conflicting parties. In Western countries – I refer specifically to Italy for obvious informational reasons – judges may behave in such a way as to pursue their own personal interests rather than act as keepers of the keeper.

This assumption seems to contrast, at least *prima facie*, with Brennan and Lomasky's (1993) thesis according to which choices in the political market – which *lato sensu* include also the selection mechanisms of constitutional judges – drastically differ from those on the economic market, which is the only place wherein individuals can make their choices with fully instrumental purposes. This Brennan and Lomasky vision, which also contrasts with standard Public Choice, when read in light of the compound symmetry approach, ends up by expanding the standard Public Choice model.

Yet though Brennan and Lomasky clearly distinguish market choices from political choices (price vs. vote), they fail to see that what really explains most of the difference between market and political choices is the number of the decision makers involved. This is the strong suit of the problem. And this element deserves more attention than is paid in the literature. My basic assumption is that when in the voting market decision makers are few, the individual's behaviour closely resembles that followed in market choices because each individual perceives himself as if he were the median voter and, hence, decisive. Consequently his choice is instrumental and not expressive. If this is true, the Brennan–Lomasky vision that expressive preferences replace instrumental behaviour in voting choices keeps its entire explanatory power only in the face of large numbers. Consequently, the *quis custodiet ipsos custodes* issue is as central as ever it was in standard Public Choice when numbers are small.

The separation of powers makes room for the keeper's keeper and yet, having to scrutinize his role and the impact of his behaviour, it is not something that is foreseeable *ex ante*. It is precisely for this reason that I have opted to refer to the facts and deeds of a specific constitutional court – the Italian Constitutional Court – to sharpen the analytical points and make them clearer. In the setting of a unitary state, the assignment of competences does not involve the distinction between separation and division of powers because the aim is that of preventing absolutism. As is well-known, Montesquieu's theory of the separation of powers was of the horizontal kind and calibrated on a single-level government, thus it concerned a single constitutional court.[11]

A N A R C H Y	Rousseau	Men-angels	No scarcity	Order without rules	No state	No guardian	Absence of moral
	Hobbes	*Homo lupus*	Scarcity	Disorder	Social contract ⇩		
				U N D I V I D E D P O W E R	Leviathan as ruler	Leviathan as the last guardian	SILENT moral discrimination
					Machiavelli's Prince	Prince as the last guardian	EXPLICIT moral discrimination
				S E P A R A T E D P O W E R	Constitutional Court and the emergence of the *quis custodiet* problem		Moral equality
					Divided power (feudalism)	Emperor as the last guardian	EXPLICIT moral discrimination

Figure 3.2   The quis custodiet *problem. An orientation map*

The distinction between separation and division of powers, championed also by Brennan and Hamlin (2000), is proper of a federal setting. The feature of a federal state, where there is a vertical division between state and federal governments, has constitutional origin and coverage. By contrast, in unitary states constitutions delegate ordinary law to institute local governments, including regional governments.

The division of powers operates along a vertical line (see Figure 3.2). Accordingly, its natural setting is a federal organisation where multiple levels of government are created by the constitutions and multiple constitutional courts. In this scheme, the division of powers can be conceived as a subset of the separation of powers. There seems to be a logical consistency in this reading, although historically it is somewhat controversial. A case in point is feudalism, whose governing body could well be defined as formally divided because vassals, vavasours and vassals of vavasours had competences over specific territories, but in reality power was unseparated. In the absence of a separation of powers, the vertical division of powers was tantamount to having a more complex and hierarchical form of Leviathan that created a situation in which nobody could check the emperor.

More to the point, it is interesting to extend the Smithian theory of the division of labour, which produces workers' specialisation, to the political–constitutional setting. The separation of powers leads to specialisation and, hence, the choice of whether to specialise in the political market or in the judicial market critically depends on a personal bent. In this way, politicians will be more inclined to pursue the public good and judges to check that the dictates of the constitution are safeguarded. For this to be feasible, one should prefigure different criteria of choice: election for politicians and appointment for judges. At this juncture, two issues are at stake: (i) that of defining who is entitled to appoint the judges of the constitutional court, and (ii) that of fixing the appointment criteria able to identify the individuals endowed with a personal bent for the judicial activity, that is, less inclined to pursue their own personal interest. On the first point, one could suggest, at least in theory, that if the constitutional judge is appointed for a single non-renewable term, the judges in office themselves might be entitled to appoint their successors. One would contend, however, that this mechanism would end up by making the constitutional court an unaccountable body: a sort of self-feeding machine. Nevertheless, this procedure would assure the independence of the constitutional court from other potential players, government included. If, instead, as happens in Italy, judges are appointed by the government *lato sensu*, the judges' independence cannot be taken for granted. Even within the compound symmetry assumption, where extreme behaviour is excluded, safeguarding the constitution may become for the judges a second best *vis à vis* their personal interests. Thus, if the judges were to deliver verdicts according to their personal interests, they ought to give up their role of checking the government. This is tantamount to saying that judges' instrumental behaviour motivated by expectation of reciprocation paves the way to obtain post-judicial appointments. Even assuming that judges are capable of shunning egoism[12] – a condition that is incompatible with the compound symmetry perspective – their trust relationship with the government lessens their reliability as keepers. Still more, an untrustworthy keeper of the constitution exposes the separation of powers to the risk of falling back to Leviathan since the constitutional court, whose aim is that of checking that the government does not violate the constitution, tames the constitution to favour the government. The consequence is that the government acquires an incongruous discretionary power to circumvent the constitution.

THE ITALIAN CONSTITUTIONAL COURT. A THIRD PLAYER OR A THIRD PARTY?

Much of the energy of the Italian Constitutional Court has gone into a search for balancing good law and policy goals. The Court's treatment of

art. 81 and the so-called 'little laws' (leggine) is enlightening in the com-
prehension of such a scenario. Article 81 of the Constitution can be encap-
sulated in two points:

1. With the budgetary law, larger or new expenditures cannot be passed;
2. The introduction of larger or new expenditures is contingent upon the
    indication of the appropriate covering means.

In this connection, art. 74 of the Constitution stipulates that the President
of the Republic can send back bills on the grounds of the absence of indication of covering instruments. Until the mid-1960s the debate was carried
out on a theoretical basis between advocates and opponents of art. 81.
At that abstract level, there was no room for any intervention by the
Constitutional Court. The Constitutional Court was involved only from
1966. Through a series of judgements the Court came to the conclusion that
resorting to debt was an appropriate means of financing. In this way the sup-
posedly protecting constraints that were intended to bind Government and
Parliament were loosened.

To define debt as an appropriate means of coverage is equal to the can-
cellation of all limits regarding expenditures; in so doing the Court's judges
grant that the benchmark of the spending laws be raised. It could be said
that the Court rebukes the legislator for 'omission' rather than 'commis-
sion'. It is patently clear that under the camouflage of the generality principle the Court gives a constitutional coverage to a deficit spending policy.
Formally the Court appeals to the generality principle to eliminate any
form of discrimination. In reality, when the Court charges Government
and Parliament of not having pursued their advantage, it resorts to an inappropriate and deceitful extension of the generality principle as the case of
the 'little laws' shows.

The 'little laws' are discretionary or derogatory rules: Government and
Parliament take these decisions to favour particular groups which are con-
centrated, well organised and politically visible. Being spending laws, 'little
laws' are subject to the coverage constraints provided in art. 81 to avoid the
risk that the President of the Republic may send back the bill to the
Parliament. In order to elude art. 81, most of the spending laws approved
by the Parliament are in reality 'little laws', and so the Government manages
to find the covering funds in the budget. Of course, this is feasible only
within certain limits. The Government well knows that once a 'little law' is
approved, the Court's judges manage to place constitutional gloss on it.
Judges, in fact, own all the instruments to complete the 'little laws', as for
instance the generality principle that is used as a cover for making them
non-discriminatory. The Court's accomplishment ends here since it is not

its duty to find the covering funds required. But the Court's judges have done more in favour of the Government. The judges' creative interpretation on matter of debt financing leaves the Government free from any coverage binds. In this sense, the lure of a post-judicial appointment induces the Court's judges to behave as legislators or co-legislators of last resort on the matter of spending laws.

To add further evidence to this stance, it is instructive to mention that up to the mid-1990s the Court had never made controls on the legitimacy of decree laws including decree laws that had been re-issued. If the Court's judges aimed at reviewing rather than pursuing their own private interest (art. 134, see also art. 77 of the Constitution), re-issuance of decree laws would be hardly justifiable. Only in 1993 did the Court judge all re-issued decree laws unconstitutional. It is reasonable to think that this has not happened by pure chance. In fact, in 1993 the political sponsors who had appointed those judges were no longer in office since parties had been wound up as a consequence of the 'Clean Hands' corruption investigation. Hence judges were no longer dependent on the politicians for their post-tenure appointment, and started to judge differently from the preceding 37 years – for example on the matter of referendum admissibility, on electoral matters, and the unconstitutionality of re-issued decree laws. At this time, judges behaved as a third party. This particular case, which is purely incidental, strongly suggests that the Achilles' heel of the Constitutional Court lies in the appointment procedures. The single non-renewable term is a mechanism not robust enough to insure that constitutional judges be untouched by the incentives that the government could supply after their term in office. It is, in fact, the prospect of a post-judicial career, another incentive that pushes judges to follow a 'good policy' in favour of the government.

Of course, an appointment for life for the Court's judges, as for the US Supreme Court's justices, would eliminate the collusive behaviour induced by the lure of a post-judicial office. Yet the appointment for life is not the only alternative, and it might have some contra-indications. Judges might be pushed by gratitude to support choices taken by the government that has appointed them and consequently might oppose decisions taken by the government in office, if it is different from that which has appointed them, just because they do not run the risk of losing their office. To eliminate the post-judicial incentive, a list of all potential eligible judges – all those who meet the requirement of art. 135 of the Constitution – could be drafted, and whenever the judge's term expires the new judge could be chosen by drawing lots.

CONCLUSIONS

If the criterion followed in the appointment of judges is that of making reference to their past as ordinary men in order to foresee their future behaviour as judges, one may make highly erroneous evaluations. That is why I assume, in line with Brennan, that the judges of the constitutional court are neither better, nor worse, than all other citizens. The altruistic component pushes the judge towards the accomplishment of his duty of controlling, while the egoistic component drives him to please the government to ensure a return in terms of post-judicial appointments. Because of the restricted number of judges, the latter component tends to prevail so that judges behave in a translucent manner and can recognise their mutual advantage. This means that the judges of the constitutional court vote instrumentally rather than expressively. An instrumental usage of the vote and the hope of post-judicial reward sap the judge's role of keeper: instead of serving as a referee he behaves as a team-mate. Yet more, when the controlled conditions the controller, it is by no means the judge's role as a third party alone that collapses, but also the moral equality among individuals as resulting from the separation of powers.

The incentives of the judges of the constitutional court make both the executive and the judicial power not so separated and this does not warrant an equal treatment for the agents on the grounds of constitutional rules. Despite the formal separation of powers, the moral equality of the agents is undermined by the judges' incentives to side with governments to create a net of privileges. The example of the Italian Constitutional Court shows that it is precisely the body that was originally designated to control the government that dramatically ends up by making the *quis custodiet ipsos custodes* problem a perennial one. Although not expressly attributing the reason to constitutional courts, Tullock (2004) has recently asserted, on the basis of historical evidence, that democracies sooner or later may result in dictatorship. In light of Tullock's reasoning, the constitutional court might play a non-negligible role in the potential failure of the separation of powers, which is supposed to be the safest foundation for moral equality of individuals in a democratic system.

Brennan's position, based on methodological individualism whose motivational elements I have embodied in my compound symmetry, leads to a less pessimistic evaluation than the one pictured by Tullock. It is precisely the moral equality resulting from the separation of powers that makes the breach of contracts and the failure in keeping faith to promises costly. For Brennan, the very existence of the constitution warrants that judges do not perceive themselves as being morally entitled to act against it. The fact should not be overlooked, however, that under a generalised corruption, there could not be any constitutional limit robust enough as to monitor general disorder. Unless one resorts to the Kantian categorical imperative, there seems to be no other barrier against the folly of the reason able to constrain behaviours within moral rules.

However, if the Kantian categorical imperative is transplanted from moral philosophy into the political and constitutional arena, the risk that it could be used to camouflage the tyranny of the majority cannot be ruled out. Should this happen, the very existence of the tyranny of the majority would indicate that the constitutional court is unable to eliminate such a risk. The only alternative that would seem to be available is that of searching for perfection. But, as Frank Knight has underlined, seeking for perfection means seeking for the impossible.

NOTES

1. Machiavelli (1882), Ch. XV, p. 51.
2. It is interesting to note the analogy with Brennan's conception of human beings. Here too individuals are moved by two elements – altruism and egoism.
3. Machiavelli (1882), Ch. XVIII, p. 58.
4. For a more complete analysis see Eusepi and Cepparulo (forthcoming).
5. Brennan (2000), p. 4.
6. In reality, Buchanan's critique of the Pigovian spurious margins is in line with the logic developed in this chapter. On this front, Cost and Choice (1969) is the most outstanding precedent of compound symmetry.
7. Brennan (2000), p. 4.
8. Eusepi and Cepparulo (forthcoming), especially sections 3 and 4.
9. See Buchanan and Tullock (1999). See also Brennan and Eusepi (2002).
10. Brennan (2000), p. 5.
11. In reality Montesquieu's theory of the separation of powers does not offer any role for the guarantor. It was not until the end of World War II, and after long and contentious debates, that a role for a control body was included in the Italian and German constitutions. Spain had a Constitutional Court at the end of the 1970s and Central and Eastern Europe after 1989. European constitutional courts have been fashioned to assimilate Kelsen's Neo-Kantian model that sharply contrasts the American model of *judicial review*. On this see Stone Sweet (2002).
12. This statement is incompatible with the logic of compound symmetry. It would require, in fact, an Aristotelian perspective according to which temptations have no impact on individual behaviours, being individuals predetermined from birth.

REFERENCES

Brennan, G. (2000), 'Trust adjudication and the *quis custodiet* problem', typescript.
Brennan, Geoffrey and Loren Lomasky (1993), *Democracy and Decision. The Pure Theory of Electoral Preference*, Cambridge, UK and New York, USA: Cambridge University Press.

Brennan, Geoffrey and Alan Hamlin (2000), *Democratic Devices and Desires*, Cambridge, UK and New York, USA: Cambridge University Press.

Brennan, G. and G. Eusepi (2002), 'Buchanan, Hobbes and Contractarianism: The supply of rules?', paper presented at the Public Choice Meeting, San Diego, CA, USA, April 2001.

Buchanan, James M. (1969), *Cost and Choice: An Inquiry in Economic Theory*, Chicago: Markham Publishing Company.

Buchanan, James M. (1975), *The Limits of Liberty: Between Anarchy and Leviathan*, Chicago: University of Chicago Press.

Buchanan, James M. and Gordon Tullock (1962), *The Calculus of Consent. Logical Foundations of Constitutional Democracy*, reprinted (1999), in J.M. Buchanan *The Collected Works of James M. Buchanan*, **3** Indianapolis: Liberty Fund.

Buchanan, James M. and Gordon Tullock (1999), 'Appendix 1', *Marginal Notes on Reading Political Philosophy*, pp. 305–25.

Eusepi, G. and A. Cepparulo (forthcoming), 'Variations on the lupus et agnus story. In search of the homo sapiens', in A. Marciano and J.M. Josselin (eds), *Democracy, Freedom and Coercion: A Law and Economics Approach*, Cheltenham, UK and Northampton, MA, USA: Edward Elgar.

Frey, Bruno, S. (1997), *Not Just for the Money. An Economic Theory of Personal Motivation*, Cheltenham, UK and Brookfield, USA: Edward Elgar.

Kliemt, H. (2004), 'The morals of power politics or better in the West', in Geoffrey Brennan (ed.), *Coercive Power and Its Allocation in the Emergent Europe*, *Rivista di Politica Economica*, **XCIV** (VII–VIII), 159–88.

Machiavelli, Niccolò (1882), *The Historical, Political, and Diplomatic Writings of Niccolò Machiavelli*, translated from the Italian by Christian E. Detmold, in four volumes, Boston: James R. Osgood and Co.

Stone Sweet, A. (2002), 'Constitutional courts and parliamentary democracy', *West European Politics*, **25** (1), 77–100.

Tullock, G. (2004), 'On voting', paper presented at the European Center for the Study of Public Choice seminar series, Rome, Italy, June 4.

4. A bouquet of democracies

Gordon Tullock

INTRODUCTION

Governments called democracies vary a great deal. Since Australia in a number of ways is an outlier, it seems suitable to include a discussion of the different types of democracy in a collection that pays tribute to Australia's most prominent public choice scholar. There are many students of democracy who do not appreciate how many different arrangements are listed as democratic.

Governments we call democracies all depend on votes. But the nature of the dependence, and the nature of the votes varies widely. Looking at the long reach of history, it has been an unusual but by no means unknown method of government. The Epic of Gilgamesh refers in passing to a council of some sort which apparently had at least some control over the hereditary king. How many sat on this council and how it was selected are unknown, but it can be said that the oldest known civilization, Sumer, had at least some democratic aspects. There is a gap between them and what we call the classical age. Not only were Greece and Rome governed in a more or less democratic way, but there were many other governments, such as Carthage, in which an elected council of some sort was very important in the government.

THE FRANCHISE

Many governments permitted only a small group of people to vote. Athens or Rome, to name two outstanding exceptions, permitted all citizens who personally went to the place where the votes were to be counted to cast a vote there. But this type of government is now long dead and most modern governments permit practically everyone within their jurisdiction to vote in many geographical locations. Foreigners who happen to be inside the country are normally not permitted to vote and in some cases other groups, the insane or convicted criminals, for example, are banned from voting.

The serene Republic of Venice, which by almost any measure is the most successful government of history, permitted only about 5 per cent of the adult males actually living in Venice to vote. Their accomplishments include converting a sand bar into a beauty spot, building a sizable empire both in Italy and the Middle East, and protecting Europe from the Turkish navy. Culturally not only did they support the Renaissance in a way which any visitor admires, but they were also important in introducing printing and producing a large number of books. In addition, both Galileo and Vesalius were professors in their university. Thus restricted voting is not obviously a bad thing in terms of the outcomes it generates.

In modern democracies all adult citizens not insane or (in some cases) felons are permitted to vote, although, of course, not all of them will do so. Australia is unusual in making non-voting illegal. However, the word adult is not necessarily self-explanatory. The minimum voting age was 25 in prewar Japan. In Iran at the moment it is 15. During World War II a small tribe overrun by American troops in the islands decided to adopt democracy and permitted anyone over the age of 10 to vote. There was a general tradition among the English speaking nations that males became citizens at the age of 21. When the American Constitution was amended to give women the vote it was provided that they became adults for voting purposes at the age of 18. This sexual oddity attracted no attention until the 1980s at which point both Congress and the Supreme Court took action to make males adults – for purposes of voting – at the age of 18.[1]

In general women were not permitted to vote anywhere until the 20th century. Imperial Germany was the first country to have full general female voting in 1911. New Zealand allowed women to vote – but not to stand as candidates – from 1893, and widows could vote in Canada from 1883. Finland, then part of Russia, introduced female suffrage in 1906. Switzerland was, I think, the last significant democratic country to permit general voting by women.[2] In addition, it is very hard to become a Swiss citizen and 'guest workers', who make up 25 per cent of the workers in Switzerland, cannot vote.

ENGLISH ORIGINS

The whole problem of who can vote is historically complex. The restriction to male citizens who actually made it to a large area where voters assembled was common in classical civilization, but this idea is now dead except for a few town meetings. A brief history of the development of voting in England will indicate how complex the matter is. Under feudalism the army of the King was actually composed of his noblemen and their personal followers. Given these circumstances the King was wise to consult with his noblemen before going to war. In one of the many civil wars which distracted England,

Warwick, the leader of the revolt, asked each city or county in England to send two knights to consult with him. After Warwick was beaten, the King decided to retain the custom and hence the English House of Commons was born.

There were thus two councils in England, the Lords and the Commons, descending from this particular revolt. The system was, however, extremely corrupt with many of the seats in the House of Commons being owned by people who sat in the Lords. To take one extreme example Old Sarum was a plowed field which sent two representatives to the Commons.[3] Since the British Prime Minister during much of the war with the French under Napoleon sat for Old Sarum, the system cannot be said to have failed.

As further evidence that this bizarre system was not totally worthless, not only did it defeat Napoleon, but it also presided over the Industrial Revolution. The reforms of 1842 made the House of Commons a genuinely elected body although it was elected by only a part of the adult male population. The number of people who could vote was increased steadily until 1928 when the last small group of females finally got the vote. In 1890 when the number of people permitted to vote was still less than the entire male population, England had the highest per capita income in the world. As the franchise has been extended England has lost ground on this particular measure, although whether this is an example of cause-and-effect or merely coincidence, I have no way of testing.

There is one peculiar characteristic of the extension of the franchise to subjects of the English King. There was never any discussion at all[4] of simply extending the franchise to those subjects of the King Emperor who lived in places like India. The same restriction on the extension of the democratic voting rights applies to the other imperial powers. I think there is an easy explanation, but since this explanation implies that democratic voters are not willing to share their wealth with other people, I am uncertain as to whether it is the true solution. Most modern democratic governments, in order to please their voters, transfer much money from their wealthiest minority to the less wealthy majority. Since the inhabitants of colonial India vastly outnumbered the inhabitants of Great Britain and had much less money, giving them a vote for the House of Commons would have led to very large transfers of money, not from a wealthy Englishman to the poor Englishman, but from all Englishmen to the much poorer and much more numerous subjects of the King Emperor living in India. The extension of the franchise within England benefited a clear majority of the inhabitants in England, even if it did not benefit the wealthy minority, most of whom were permitted to vote even before the extension.

The extension took place in relatively small steps and, in general, the parties that carried out each step gained in the next election. They certainly would not have gained had they admitted the Indians to the vote. The same phenomena will be seen elsewhere. The French revolutionary assembly took measures to make certain that the vote was restricted to the upper classes. They thought that the lower classes were basically royalist and had to be kept out of power. Indeed Napoleon achieved his power to a large extent because he was the only general in the French army who was willing to order the artillery to fire into a Parisian mob. His nephew became Emperor after he led a cavalry charge into the grandchildren of the mob destroyed by Napoleon.

AUSTRALIA

In Australia people are legally required to vote and the law is actually fairly well enforced. Geoff Brennan has expressed strong support for this legal system. He pointed out, correctly of course, that the people who do not vote in places like the United States, or indeed in most democracies, may well have different opinions from those who do vote. Thus, requiring every-one to vote might on occasion lead to a different and in one sense more 'representative' outcome. He appeared to believe that this would be a supe-rior outcome, or at least more in accord with public opinion.

I cannot disagree with the view that requiring everyone to vote would produce an outcome closer to the desires of a majority of the citizens than permitting those who don't want to vote to abstain. On the other hand, it overrides the preferences of a large number of voters who would rather not bother to go to the polls. Since I myself do not vote because I feel that the likelihood of being run over while crossing the street to get to the polling booth from my apartment is higher than the likelihood that I will change the outcome, I regard compulsory voting as oppressive. Geoff obviously does not.

Leaving aside the problems of personal preference, are there any other arguments on the issue? No one so far as I know has made a careful study of the difference between the outcomes where voting is compulsory and those in places where voting is voluntary. I am an admirer of Switzerland and tend to think that its voters do exceptionally well, but those who live in Cantons where voting is compulsory do not, so far as I know, do better than those who live in Cantons where it is voluntary. Certainly no one has ever proved that the Australian government runs better, or worse, than the run-of-the-mill democracy.

The second unusual characteristic of Australian democracy is that they use the Hare system of proportional representation. In order to protect myself from the readers in most countries, thinking I just made this up, the following description is quoted from the *Encyclopedia Americana*

The voter marks first, second, third and other choices. Election is based on a quota determined by the following formula: The total vote cast is divided by the number of seats to be filled plus one, and one is added to the quotient. If 100,000 votes are cast and 4 seats are to be filled, divide by 5 to get a quotient of 20,000 then add 1 to get 20,001, which is the quota. A candidate receiving the quota of first choice votes is elected. Surplus votes are counted for second choices, thus adding to the totals of other candidates. When other candidates reach the quota, their surpluses are distributed to later choices. The next calculation is to drop the lowest candidate and distribute his votes to the next choices marked. When the required number to reach the quota is reached, the counting terminates. A party with a very popular candidate does not, under this system, waste votes beyond his quota, for the excess votes are distributed – probably to others in his party. Votes far down the scale are not wasted because the successive elimination of party members allows one man to be elected provided the total concentration reaches the quota.[5]

Note that combined with the Australian system of compulsory voting, which is interpreted as meaning that you must list all the candidates in order of your preference, this leads to some peculiar results. It is possible, although not likely, that a candidate who you detest and hence put far down your list will receive your vote because your votes for more preferred candidates have all been eliminated in the sorting process. It is also possible for parties to make agreements among themselves as to the advice given to their voters as to whom to rank at the bottom of the list. In addition, it used to take a long time to count the ballots, but with computers that problem has been eliminated.

Whether the citizens value the vote a great deal is non-obvious. With a couple of exceptions, Sweden for example, people turn out heavily when the vote is first extended to them, but then the number turning out to vote declines with time. The fact that the majority of American voters does not bother to vote may be a good measure of the importance of democracy to the individual citizen. Almost no voters follow the advice of their high school civics teacher and become well informed voters by heavy study. This is understandable, but discouraging for advocates of democracy as a form of government.

Leaving the Hare method aside, most democratic voting schemes for national governments can be roughly divided into two general categories: proportional representation, which is the most common form; and what I call the English system, which we use. There is also the possibility of letting the voters choose policies by directly voting on them. This is used a great deal in Switzerland and some western American states, particularly California.

PROPORTIONAL REPRESENTATION

Beginning with the proportional representation system we might use Israel as an example since they use the simplest version. Each party produces a list of candidates with as many names as the openings in the Legislature to be filled. In Israel that is the entire lower house. The voters then select a party and the seats are allocated to that party in the same proportion as their percentage of the popular vote. Since the party committee can change the ranking on the list of individual candidates for the next election, this leads to very stringent party discipline. In Israel there are, in essence, two major parties on the right and left and then parties which represent orthodox religious groups. Frequently, neither of the major parties acquires a majority and hence governments tend to be coalitions with the religious parties being paid off by appropriations for their school system and other religious activities. Put the other way around, the religious parties, which attract minority vote shares, actually carry considerable political power.

Most of the countries which use proportional representation do not use a single national electoral district but break the country up into several areas, each of which sends a number of representatives to the Legislature. These representatives are divided among the parties proportion to their votes. Sometimes the voters have influence over which particular members of the given party represent a particular constituency, but this is not universal.

Switzerland has an ingenious variant in which individual voters are permitted to draw a line through one of the names on the list and write in one of the others so that a particular voter can cast two votes for his favorite candidate. When seats are allocated to the party, the individuals who received the most votes are selected first and then the remainders of the number elected from that constituency are selected in the usual manner.

It turns out that only rather small minorities of the Swiss voters choose to go to the trouble of doing this and hence the individual members of the Legislature are selected by a rather small number of voters. Further, in general there are few precautions in Switzerland to keep the vote secret. As a result the elected candidate may well know the names of the rather small number of voters who cumulated for him and hence ensured his election.

As a general rule, countries which use this type of electoral system have a Legislature of two houses but the upper house is generally much the weaker. Sweden has recently abolished the upper house and hence has only one legislative chamber. Normally, although there are exceptions, no single party acquires a majority in the lower and more powerful house. The executive is not separately elected but formed by the parties controlling the lower house. This normally, although not always, means that it is a coalition of several parties because no single party has gained enough seats to get a majority.

Anthony Downs, in his pioneering work, criticized this system of proportional representation very severely on the grounds that the individual voter could not tell at the time of the election what particular coalition of parties would be formed after the election was over. Thus, in Downs' view, he could not cast an informed vote because he did not know – and could not know – what government he was voting for. I always objected to this line of reasoning because although the voter does not know what coalition will be formed his vote conveys more information to the political process than in the two-party system. There doesn't seem to be any empirical way of deciding who is right on this.

SIMPLE MAJORITIES

In most other democracies, members of the Legislature are elected by a straight majority vote in a single constituency. A Congressman is nominated for a particular district and becomes a member of Congress if he gets more votes than anyone else. Sometimes there are rules that there is a run-off if no single member gets a majority of votes.

England here is something of a special case. Since the 1920s, they have had three major parties, Labour, Conservative, and Liberal (now Liberal-Democrat), operating with a first-past-the post electoral system. As a result of this system, no peacetime government elected in England since the 1920s has attracted a majority of the popular vote, even though a number of governments have won large overall majorities in the House of Commons. In the 2005 election, the Labour party won the election with a fairly comfortable majority of 66 seats in the House of Commons with just 46 per cent of the popular vote.

The peculiarity of this system is not much noted. Government switches from time to time between the Conservative and Labour parties with the Liberal-Democrats a distant third, but in a simple two-party election it is quite possible that the Liberal-Democrats could beat either of the other two parties. Given a choice between a Liberal-Democrat and Labour, most Conservative voters would vote Liberal-Democrat. Given a choice between Liberal-Democrat and Conservative, most Labour voters would vote Liberal-Democrat. Thus, a party which is quite probably a Condorcet winner – in that it could get a clear majority against either of the other two parties – is normally relegated to a minor role in British politics. In any event, one cannot call Britain an example of majority rule in terms of the popular vote. As far as I know, Britain is the only country which has this problem in a major way.

PRESIDENTIAL SYSTEM

The model of the United States, a pioneer, has been followed in most of the American continent where they have a democratic government. In this system there is only one person elected for each constituency or office. The parties nominate candidates in each legislative constituency and for the President. Normally there are only two and one therefore gets a majority. When there are more than two and no one gets a majority, either the one with the most votes is elected or there is some kind of run-off. Since this system is used to select the Legislature there is a powerful practical reason for believing there will be only two parties in the Legislature and one of them will have a majority there. Although there is no guarantee that the party with the greater share of the popular vote in a country as a whole will necessarily hold a majority of seats in the Legislature, that does tend to be the outcome.

The United States, the pioneer of this particular type of government, has a powerful President who not only runs the executive branch but has veto power which gives him considerable legislative influence. One can say that there are three houses of the Legislature in this kind of government, all three elected by majority voting[6] and one of them being a single man. Other than in the United States, this system has not worked terribly well. In South America, for a long time, democracy alternated with dictatorships. At the moment all South American countries except Cuba and Haiti are democratic although some of them are showing signs of returning to the previous alternation of democracy and dictatorship.

It should be noted that this system in essence requires more than a majority of voters to pass any particular bill. Since the two houses are elected differently and the President by yet a third way, a bare majority of the population is not likely to be able to control all three of these bodies. Exactly how many votes are necessary to obtain a majority in each house and a concurring President (or a sufficient majority in both houses to overturn a Presidential veto) is not obvious, but it is obviously more than a bare majority of the voters.

There is another peculiarity of the American system which we share in full only with Iran. In both of these countries a group of elderly and learned men are permitted to veto democratically passed legislation and, in fact, may order government action which has not passed the legislative process. In both cases these learned men are engaged in enforcing a previous system of jurisprudence. In both cases, in fact, these learned men from time to time change and add to this previously existing jurisprudence. The Iranian Council of Guardians has considerably more power than the American Supreme Court. It can and does rule that certain candidates for elective office are ineligible. I believe that it is more active in giving positive orders to the government to take actions of various sorts than is the Supreme Court, although the rulings made by the Supreme Court and subordinate courts with respect to desegregation are strong enough that this judgment may not be reliable.

It can be seen from the above catalogue that democracy is not a specific form of government but a category of government which allows a good deal of internal variety. Its distinguishing feature is that the government depends to at least some extent on votes of the citizens. In many of the above listed cases, only a part of the people we would now consider as voters were permitted to vote in many democratic situations. Further, calling it a majority system is misleading. England, as we have mentioned, normally elects a government with less than a majority of voters on its side. Both Kennedy and the second Bush received less than the number of votes cast for their principal opponent. When the candidates of the two principal parties are close, it is not unusual for there to be enough votes cast for the minor parties so that the winner does not receive a majority of the total votes cast.

When proportional representation is used, as it is in many democracies, the coalition put together normally has a majority of the votes, but no individual party does. I have already mentioned above Anthony Downs' objections to this system, which is that the voter does not know the government he is supporting until after the coalition is formed, and hence necessarily cannot vote for the government which he prefers because at the time of the vote it doesn't exist.

HISTORY

At the time of writing, about half of the world's population lives under democratic government of one type or another. But a large part of this half is made up by India, and I don't think anybody thinks that India has had a very successful government in recent years. Further, for much of its history it was dominated by one family. I do not think that this means it could have been called a hereditary monarchy, but it clearly had some resemblance to one.

The United Nations sometimes refers to itself as a democracy. It does depend on votes, but these votes are cast by governments and at the moment non-democratic governments in places like Africa and the Middle East have a clear majority in the assembly. Further, these seats are allocated one to each nation, without regard to population. The Security Council, which acts as an upper house, has five permanent members, who are simply the winning coalition of World War II. Since these great powers all have vetoes, this can hardly be referred to as a majority voting system.

In practice the United States rarely uses its veto and in fact has almost always used it not for the benefit of the United States, but for the benefit of Israel. Here is a case where the leaders of what at the time was called the democratic world chose against majority voting. Since the rulers of Russia and China were not democrats themselves, it is not surprising that the outcome was not democratic. It seems to me dubious, however, that the United States would have accepted simple majority vote of the nations even if it had been proposed.

Today almost everyone is in favor of democratic government. Before evaluating it, we should look a little bit at its history. Both Greek and Roman democracy failed. Although the Roman Empire was a rather good government in general, and used democratically controlled city states as constituent units, it was, after all, a monarchy. The German tribes which destroyed the Roman Empire had domestic arrangements of a somewhat democratic character before they seized Western Europe. In general, however, the states they set up were monarchies. In the Middle East, Asia, and the local civilizations in the Americas before Columbus, we find no democracies.

Ironically, and surprisingly, less of the world is controlled by democratic governments today than was the case before World War II. During the 19th century democratic governments in countries like France, England, the Netherlands, and Belgium conquered most of the non-European world. Whether we should say that India before World War II was part of a democracy or not depends on the exact usage of words. I think that few people would classify it as democratic even though it was controlled by the voters in England. Today, of course, it is democratic, although subject to the criticisms I have presented above. Other parts of the former European empires have tended to fall into temporary and unpleasant dictatorships. Consider the Congo. Before World War II it was ruled by a democratic government, but not one selected by the Congolese. Since then it has alternated between dictatorship and chaos.

The former area controlled by Russia has disintegrated and most of the parts in Europe are currently democratic, although in my opinion this democracy is most insecure. That part of the former Russia which used to be called 'Russian Turkestan' has mainly become dictatorial. The central government also seems to be in the process of going from a democratic to an autocratic government, but we cannot, of course, be sure.

CONCLUSION

These are statements as to what is happening, but can we evaluate it? At the moment most of the most prosperous nations of the world are democracies, although Singapore and Hong Kong are outstanding exceptions. Historically speaking, however, the prosperous democracies were prosperous before World War II when some of them were emphatically not democratic. It would appear that prosperity depends on something other than form of government.

Altogether I have given a sort of dictionary of democratic governments. Most people who live in the United States, Australia, or other such countries will regard the view that possibly democracy is not the best form of government as absurd. Those who are members of the Public Choice Society are particularly likely to think that democracy is the best form of government. We should note, however, that the Public Choice Society does not select its president or the members of its board democratically. So far that has not led to disaster.

But what is it about democracy that makes it seem such a self-evidently good thing both to many ordinary citizens and to many students of politics? What aspect of democracy is it that generates this confident faith? Given the variety of democracies sketched here it will be difficult to find any very plausible answer to this question other than some very general statement to the effect that voters retain the right to 'throw the scoundrels out'. It may be that the perceived value of democracy lies not so much in the additional prosperity that democracies may enjoy (if indeed this is the case) but rather in the fact that democracy seems to offer intrinsic value to citizens. On this view, democracy might seem a little like a luxury that countries can afford once they reach a certain level of general affluence. Of course, this would then open up the question of how much of a trade-off there might be between the perceived benefits of living in a democratic society and the productive benefits of some other form of government, that might include some limited elements of democracy. It may be that the contrast between China and the western democracies over the coming years will provide an interesting case study on this matter.

I find that this chapter is rather unsatisfactory. It is a description of forms of government which most of my readers will be moderately familiar with. It doesn't really evaluate them, although I could offer my own opinion that Singapore, a hereditary monarchy, seems to be doing very well indeed. If we look over the long sweep of history, that has been the standard form of government. I think most of my readers will both hope and believe that we are now entering into another epoch in which democracy, of one sort or another, will control the world. I share that hope, but do not feel safe in making any predictions.

NOTES

1. The change was obviously within the constitutional power of the Legislature, but the Supreme Court, in ruling that constitutionally men must be permitted to vote from 18 on, was clearly engaging in its modern habit of amending the Constitution. All the people who wrote the Constitution came from states where the voting age was 21.
2. Portugal allowed full female suffrage only in 1976 – prior to that date there were restrictions relating to the level of education. Liechtenstein allowed female suffrage only in 1984.
3. Namier's 'The Structure of English Government at the Accession of George III' is a most amusing account of the way various people got into the House.
4. Or at least none that I can discover.
5. *Encyclopedia Americana*, vol. 19, p. 210, 1969.
6. The voters, strictly speaking, vote for members of the college of electors who then elect the President. In two cases this century, Kennedy and the second Bush, the candidate who got the most popular votes did not have a majority in the college. Jefferson beat Adams in 1800 although Adams had more popular votes. States with slaves were given additional votes in the Electoral College.

PART II

Searching for stability in democracy

5. Subjective evaluation of alternatives in individual voting choice

James M. Buchanan and Yong J. Yoon

INTRODUCTION

The aim in this chapter is to clarify some ambiguities that remain in social choice theory more than a half century after Arrow's seminal proof of his impossibility theorem (Arrow, 1951). Specifically, why did Arrow, along with his critics and interpreters, restrict analysis to constructions based only on ordinal utility rankings? Relatedly, why have social choice theorists, generally, presumed that persons' *primitive* preference orderings over collectively determined outcomes become the appropriate benchmark from which postulates for rationality in individual voting choice are assessed?[1] Finally, how will a relaxation of the ordinality restriction affect analyses of collective action?

In the second and third sections we address the first question: Why the restriction to ordinal rankings? In short, the economists' escape from utilitarianism was overextended, while, at the same time, economists sought to derive normative criteria for collective action rather than explain such action in itself. In the fourth section, we re-examine the categorical distinction between individual choice behaviour in the market and in voting – a distinction that is familiar but the full implications of which have never been properly understood. The fifth, sixth and seventh sections concentrate on individual voting choice in stylized examples in which differences among collective outcomes are ordered and, in some settings, cardinalized, with emphasis on the critical importance of information concerning the preferences of other voters. The eighth section argues that all voting is strategic in a properly defined sense. Section nine concludes the chapter.

UTILITARIANISM AND ECONOMIC THEORY

With the exceptions of some of the Italians, notably Barone and Pareto, economists of the first third of the twentieth century were almost universally utilitarian, in the classic definitional sense. Utility, as such, was measurable, interpersonally comparable and, hence, aggregatable. And, importantly, utility offered a meaningful criterion upon which political policy might be evaluated. 'To maximize aggregate utility' – to Edgeworth, Sidgwick, Marshall, and more directly, Pigou – as the normative basis for an 'economics of welfare' seemed to be well grounded.

For English-language economists, this cosy stance was shattered by Lionel Robbins in his influential small book published in 1932, *The Nature and Significance of Economic Science*, in which Robbins challenged the utilitarian dominance. He suggested that efforts to measure utility met no criteria for scientific validity, and that the inherently subjective nature of anything called 'utility' precluded any standard for interpersonal comparability. Hence, aggregation over persons was obviously impossible.

Economists were quick to join in the condemnation and to jettison utility measurement to the junk pile of failed ideas. To salvage something, however, they soon discovered Pareto, who had, early in the century, sensed that much of basic economic theory could be reestablished by using only ordinal preference rankings, that choice behaviour in markets might be satisfactorily explained with propositions that were empirically falsifiable. So long as participants in market interactions could be presumed to order separate bundles of goods (bads), a fully operational pure science of economics seemed to be restored, even if its welfare implications were drastically limited. Persons could be modelled as behaving as if they were maximizing an ordinally defined utility function. Revealed preferences, as stylized, filled in the gaps.

The welfare criterion became Pareto optimality, or efficiency, which allowed for no direct interpersonal comparability so long as persons themselves could be made the judges of their own welfare, simply defined as standing on their revealed preference ordering. The profoundly individualistic criterion of Pareto optimality replaced the profoundly collectivistic criterion of classic utilitarianism.

But how could separate individual preferences be aggregated in those naturally collectivistic settings where shared results must emerge, that is, where persons cannot choose separately and independently one from another? How could a meaningful 'social welfare function' be constructed, even if we make the heroic assumption that individual preference orderings over collective outcomes are coherent?

This question or problem is that which Kenneth Arrow posed for himself, and, as soon became familiar, he solved through his proof of the general impossibility theorem. Given the mind-set of the theoretical welfare economists of the mid-1940s, when Arrow commenced his quest, any usage of classical utilitarianism beyond ordinality would have been ruled out of court. Any dissertation effort that reintroduced the ordering of differences would have been summarily rejected. No one bothered to re-examine elements in the classical utilitarian structure that might become relevant in choices made outside the stylized buyer–seller market relationship.

The economists' blinders kept the early contributors, economists all, from realizing that the Robbins critique could not be interpreted to reject subjective utility measurement, as sensed by the individual himself, at least to the extent of allowing for the prospect that persons can order differences among the items included in the inclusive ordinal rankings and, possibly, also assign cardinalized values to the alternatives. There is nothing that prevents the individual, subjectively, from knowing that the differences between end-objects along the scale may themselves be ordered. The person who confronts the alternatives A, B and C can know whether the difference in utility between A and B is greater than, equal to or less than the difference between B and C. A moment's introspection suffices. On a cold winter's day, if there are only three settings on the thermostat: 75 degrees Fahrenheit, 65 degrees and off, the difference between the first of these two settings is surely recognized to be less than the difference between the second and third. And this result holds regardless of where the zero point is set on the temperature scale.

Acceptance of the Von Neumann–Morgenstern extension of conventional analysis to incorporate conceptually observable choices between lottery-like alternatives can be interpreted as an indirect acknowledgment of individuals' capacity to evaluate differences subjectively. There is no implication, however, to the effect that differences can be evaluated only in the presence of options that are defined probabilistically.

THE SOCIAL WELFARE FUNCTION

A second source for the apparent failure to go beyond ordinal utility in application to collective choice settings is to be found in the ambiguity concerning the ultimate purpose of the whole analytical enterprise in social choice. This ambiguity, and its implications, was discussed by Sen in his American Economic Association presidential address (Sen, 1995), where he attempted to reconcile Arrow's construction and Buchanan's critique. The Arrow question was that posed above. If we assume that individuals are described by coherent preference orderings over social states, defined as the alternatives for collective choice, how can these ordinal rankings be aggregated so as to generate a 'social' ordering that exhibits a set of seemingly reasonable properties? The question was put as if an external observer, informed by the separate individual preference orderings, was charged with the task of generating the function that would allow the result to be 'read off' in scalar fashion. 'To derive' such a function; this was the appropriately defined purpose of the effort.

In this framework, restriction to ordinal preferences over outcomes becomes plausible. Conceptually, persons reveal their underlying ordinal preferences by voting for one or the other of the separate options as presented to them in pairwise comparisons. These voting actions, this behaviour, can, again conceptually, be used as information inputs for the external observer charged with deriving the social welfare function. Standing outside the individual voting choice itself, the observer cannot 'get inside', so to speak, and see any ordering of differences, if indeed these exist. To go beyond this would be unacceptable, on grounds similar to those raised by Robbins against the classical utilitarians.

The object of the whole enterprise, however, need not be that defined as posing the task of the derivation of a social welfare function to some external observer. The object of the enterprise may, instead, be the much more straightforward one of explaining how collective outcomes emerge from a set of alternatives, as determined by individual voting choices made under specified voting rules. As in the other formulation, it becomes meaningful to assume that participants are described by coherent individualized ordering of collective outcomes. This approach requires that the analytical focus be placed on the individual participant's calculus of choice as he confronts the levers in the voting booth. And in such a setting, there is nothing that suggests an arbitrary restriction that excludes the subjective evaluation of differences. As the examples below will indicate, the presumed ability of the participant to go well beyond primitive ordinal rankings of end-objects may become analytically useful in many settings.

INDIVIDUAL CHOICE IN VOTING AND THE MARKET[2]

Concentration of economists' mind-set on market choice served to bias analysis toward neglect of the issues discussed here. In the stylized market setting, the individual confronts alternatives, all of which are within the choice set, as determined by the exogenous constraints. If A, B and C are available, the individual need only select that option which stands highest on the preference ordering. For example, if the budget permits, the consumer may purchase an apple (A), an orange (B) or a pear (C). And, once a choice is made, the end-state is immediately realized, as brought into being by the choice itself. There is a one-to-one correspondence between choice and consequence. In this stylized market setting, any possible ordering of differences becomes immaterial. The consumer may only slightly prefer the apples to the orange, while much preferring either of these to the pear. Or conversely. The order of the utility differences among the alternatives is of no consequence in explaining choice behaviour in the market. Nor is there any need to invoke cardinal measurability of utility, even as subjectively considered.

Note, however, that the objects or end-states among which market choices are made are, themselves, evaluated *locally*, that is, these enter directly as arguments in the ordinal utility function of the chooser. That is to say, the ranking is over apples, oranges and pears only. There is no presumed ordinal ranking over the 'social states', described in terms of aggregate or market-wide characteristics. An individual's choice of, say, an apple does, of course, affect the vector of prices in the economy and, ultimately, the vector of resource allocation, but no consideration is given to such effects in the calculus of choice itself. The individual in the marketplace is not making a 'social' choice.[3]

Implications of the categorical difference between market choice and voting choice has not been sufficiently incorporated into the analysis of collective action. In stylized voting choice, the individual is presumed to possess an ordinal preference ranking over the set of end-states that are properly described as 'social' or 'collective' in the sense that they both enter simultaneously into the preference orderings of other persons and are potentially available, if chosen, simultaneously to all participants in the inclusive interaction. In voting choice, the individual is necessarily evaluating 'public goods' in the classic Samuelsonian sense. There is nothing in the structure of the voting process, as stylized, which requires that the individual participant evaluate directly the choice options within his localized control, for example, the levers in the voting booth. To be fully comparable here, the individual in the market would be required to place no evaluation on apples, oranges and pears, but to concentrate attention on the overall effects of his choice behaviour. In sum, the arguments in the individual's utility function are categorically different in the two settings. In stylized market choice, the presumed utility ranking is over localized, separately confronted, 'private goods' options; in stylized voting the ranking is over 'social states' (candidates, parties, platforms, tax rates, spending patterns).

The particular descriptive features of the end-objects in the individual's utility function need not take on critical importance if the relationship between the act of choice and the consequence of choice remains invariant. It is precisely at this point, however, that the two institutional settings herein compared, the market and the voting process, become different for any calculus of individual decision. As noted, in stylized market choice, the individual directly brings into being the preferred option from among the set of alternatives confronted. In collective settings, by contrast, it is in one sense inappropriate even to use the word 'choice'. The individual may, indeed, rank order the alternatives that are evaluated, but he lacks the authority to bring any one of these alternatives directly into being. Hence, the individual does not 'choose' in the sense that selection does not generate a specific result. No one really 'chooses' the outcome, which does emerge from the separated selections made by the several (or many) participants, as amalgamated through some rule. The game theory analogy is useful here. No one chooses the outcome of the game, as such. Instead, the outcome emerges as a result of the separate actions taken by the separated but interdependent players.

The individual in a political context could be placed in a role akin to that of the individual in the market only if he is assigned a dictatorship position, in which he could indeed choose for the whole community. In all settings where the collective outcome is determined by the selections made by separate but interdependent voters, no one makes a 'social choice'.

THE RELEVANCE OF ORDERED DIFFERENCES

In all situations where the single voter cannot directly choose the collective outcome, the subjective evaluation of the end-states over which the ordinal ranking is made becomes relevant in determining whether or not the latter ranking is sufficient to explain the individual's voting behaviour. Since a vote for, say, option A does not directly ensure that A will emerge as the collective outcome, the person whose rank order is, say, ABC, may enhance the prospect of ensuring the highest possible outcome on his preference scale by voting for B or C in a presumed sequence of pairwise comparisons. There is no logical linkage between the primitive rank order over collective outcomes and the voting behaviour of the individual. There is no presumption that the primitive preference ordering is the benchmark or basis from which departures may be judged, somehow, to be insincere, dishonest or even strategic. Whether or not the primitive preference ordering will describe voting behaviour will depend on the variables to be discussed below rather than on any incoherence in the rational calculus of the individual voter.

Our central point may be illustrated by simple examples. Suppose there are three voters, 1, 2 and 3, and three alternatives, A, B and C, which voter 1, whose calculus we consider, orders in that sequence. Assume that this potential voter can order the differences, with that between A and B, less than that between B and C. That is, $[U(A) - U(B)] < [U(B) - U(C)]$. The utility profile for voter 1 is that shown as F3 in Figure 5.1. This voter's

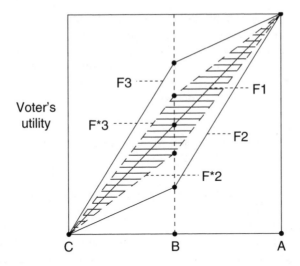

Figure 5.1   Utility profiles for reference voter

behaviour will depend on predictions about how others will vote. Suppose that he knows with certainty that voters 2 and 3 will vote in the ordinal sequences *BCA* and *CAB*. Under strict ordinal utility without an order of differences present, this pattern generates the familiar Condorcet majority cycle if the alternatives are presented in a set of pairwise voting sequences. With the ordering of differences for voter 1, as indicated here, however, his utility may be increased by voting for *B* rather than *A* in the *AB* comparison, provided that the order of the voting sequence is random or that discounting is ignored. This action will ensure that the cycle will not occur and that *B* will become the majority solution. And this voter's utility will be higher with *B* as the equilibrium and stable solution than with the cyclical sequence *ABC*. That is, $U(B) > [U(A) + U(B) + U(C)]/3$.

The converse pattern may also occur. Suppose that the utility profile is that shown by F2 in Figure 5.1, where the difference between the most preferred alternative and the second is larger than the difference between the second and third alternative. That is, $[U(A) - U(B)] > [U(B) - U(C)]$. Suppose, further, that the predicted voting patterns of voters 2 and 3 are *BAC* and *CBA*. There is no cycle if voter 1 makes his selection in accordance with his primitive ordering. Note, however, that, in this case, $U(B) < [U(A) + U(B) + U(C)]/3$. By voting for *C* in the pairwise comparison with *B*, voter 1 brings a cycle into being and thereby increases his utility.

These simple examples suggest that the presence of ordered differences among the alternatives under consideration is a necessary condition for voting behaviour to reflect departure from the primitive ordering. That is to say, if no ordering of differences could be made, if, say, the utility 'distance' between A and B should be equal to that between B and C, the inequalities in the relationships above would be replaced with equal signs. In this case, voter 1 would gain nothing by acting so as to prevent the majoritarian cycle in the first example and, similarly, gain nothing by generating the cycle in the second.

PREDICTIONS CONCERNING THE VOTING BEHAVIOUR OF OTHERS

The examples also suggest that the individual calculus of voting must incorporate predictions about the voting behaviour of other participants. With subjective evaluation of options, the individual's vote is not invariant over differing predictions about the behaviour of other voters, even if there is no strategic element involved in the sense that one's own behaviour can affect that of others.

In the simple examples introduced above, we assumed that the calculus of voter 1 is informed by perfect information about the patterns of behaviour for voters 2 and 3. The next step is to examine this calculus as the perfect information assumption is relaxed.

We may commence by shifting attention to the other end of the information spectrum – that in which the individual voter has no information at all concerning the possible voting behaviour of other participants. In this situation it is possible to demonstrate that, even if the individual is able to assign measurable utility values to the alternatives in his own preference ranking, there are no rational grounds for departing from the behaviour indicated by the primitive preference ordering (see Appendix 5A). Each of the other voters would, in this case, be assigned an equal probability of voting in accordance with each of the possible profiles.

An interesting variant on this zero information model is that in which the single voter is confronted with only two of the alternatives in a straightforward pairwise comparison, but with no knowledge as to the presence and/or future prospect of a third or more alternatives being put forward in a sequence. In this sparse setting, the individual would have no basis for voting other than in accord with his primitive ranking between the two alternatives presented. In this situation, even if the individual should have access to information concerning how others will vote, this information cannot be helpful.[4]

The cases of interest here are those that fall between the extreme limits of the information spectrum, but where the individual voter is aware that other alternatives than those presented in a specific pairwise comparison are 'out there', lurking in the wings so to speak, and ready to be tested against any current winner. In these settings, the potential voter is not totally uninformed about the behaviour of other voters, but he remains less than certain about his predictions. That is to say, he is able to assign something other than equiprobability ratings to specific profiles of other voters, but the probabilities here may range over the whole spectrum, from zero to one, excluding only these limit values. Note that, in order to predict the voting behaviour of so much as a single other voter, the person attempting such a prediction must do more than estimate the primitive preference ordering of that voter. In addition, any prediction of voting behaviour must be informed by some estimate of the shape of the preference profile, that is, the ordering of differences among the alternatives. And, further, before the potential voter can determine his own voting choice among the alternatives, as presented, he must estimate the distribution of the several possible voting orders among the whole set of participants in the collective decision process.

VOTING CHOICE WITH THREE ALTERNATIVES, THREE VOTERS UNDER PARTIAL KNOWLEDGE

A fully comprehensive analysis of individual voting choice under the presumption that differences can be ordered and subjectively evaluated would indeed be a major undertaking. We shall leave this challenge for future research and researchers. We limit discussion here to the simplest possible case that retains analytical relevance – that of three alternatives for voting choice, A, B and C, and three potential voters, 1, 2 and 3, each of whom knows the institutional setting and each of whom can subjectively evaluate the utility promised by the three collective outcomes.

We shall limit treatment to a single illustrative example. Select a reference voter, voter 1, with the primitive preference profile ABC. This person can predict, with certainty, that voter 2 will exhibit voting behaviour described by the profile BCA. Voter 1 remains, however, totally ignorant as to the voting behaviour of voter 3.

There are six possible voting profiles for voter 3: ABC, ACB, BAC, BCA, CAB and CBA. Given the known profile for voter 2, BCA, voter 1 knows that, if he votes in accordance with his primitive ordering, the equiprobable outcomes are $\{A, A, B, B, \text{Condorcet cycle}, B\}$. Given a presumed ability to evaluate the alternatives subjectively, are there preference profiles for voter 1 that would dictate voting behaviour contrary to the primitive ordering?

Consider the utility profile depicted by F3 in Figure 5.1, where the utility difference between the first and second highest alternatives is less than the difference between the second and third alternatives. Note that, by voting in accordance with the profile *BAC*, voter 1 can eliminate the one-in-six cyclical result, thereby guaranteeing against the emergence of alternative *C* altogether and generating the stable solution *B* under all configurations of voter 3's profile. In so doing, however, voter 1 will have also eliminated the two possible *A* outcomes that he would most prefer.

The indicated voting behaviour of voter 1 will clearly depend on the relative utility distances between the two sets of options. This calculus must involve not only an ordering of the differences, but also a cardinalization of the utility values. If this calculus reveals that the value or utility differential between *C* and *B* is a critical multiple of that between *A* and *B*, voter 1 can increase his utility by voting in accordance with the *BAC* profile rather than his primitive *ABC* profile.[5] The simple ordering of the differences here, that is, $[U(A) - U(B)] < [U(B) - U(C)]$ (all that was required under perfect information), is not sufficient under partial knowledge about the voting profiles of others.

In a limited sense, the analysis may be generalized by reference to the geometrical construction in Figure 5.1. Under conditions of total ignorance about how others might vote, the reference voter will exhibit voting behaviour that precisely maps his primitive preference ordering (see Appendix 5A), and this behaviour remains invariant regardless of the shape of the underlying subjective utility profile. In this setting, the reference voter's profile may be depicted as F3, F2 or any other pattern allowable by the primitive ordering, but differences among such profiles will exert no influence on behaviour.

Under conditions of perfect knowledge concerning the voting profiles of other voters, *any* differences in the utility distances between successive alternatives may generate voting behaviour that is inconsistent with the primitive preference ordering. Geometrically, any departure, in either direction, from the utility profile F1 in Figure 5.1 may dictate voting behaviour different from that suggested by the primitive ordering of alternatives.

In between these limits, for any degree of knowledge about the behaviour of other voters in the collectivity, there will exist a range of subjective utility profiles that may dictate voting behaviour that violates the primitive ordering. Consider, for illustration, the shaded area enclosed within the dotted profiles F*3 and F*2. These limits are determined by the amount of information possessed by the reference voter. If the primitive preference profile of this reference voter falls outside these limits, voting behaviour may not correspond to the ordering suggested in this base or primitive profile. If, on the other hand, the reference voter's primitive preference profile falls within the boundaries indicated, voting behaviour will not be different from that suggested by the primitive ordering.

As information about the voting behaviour is increased, the effect is to shrink the size of the shaded area in Figure 5.1, thereby reducing the prospect that the behaviour of the reference voter will be that which is predicted from knowledge of his ordinal ranking of the alternatives. Interestingly, the shrinkage of the shaded area to the line, depicted as F1, does not require that information about others' voting patterns be total.

ALL VOTING IS STRATEGIC

Conventional analysis of individual voting choice puts the cart before the horse. The individual's primitive preference ordering over possible collective outcomes is taken as the base or benchmark from which revealed voting behaviour is assessed, with departures from this ordering being interpreted, explicitly or implicitly, to be either irrational or at least faintly immoral. Voting behaviour that accords with the primitive ordering is often referred to as 'sincere', 'honest' or 'straightforward', and departures are taken to reflect efforts at concealing preferences with a view toward securing differential gains. Situations are analysed and examined in which such departures may be rational, but voting in such settings is often classified to be 'strategic', as if this is somehow to be distinguished from a standard pattern.

As the preceding sections have indicated, however, situations in which an individual will exhibit voting behaviour that corresponds with the primitive ordering of alternatives make up a highly restricted set once the supraordinal ability to evaluate such alternatives subjectively is permitted. There is no grounding for the presumption that the voting behaviour consistent with the primitive ordering should become the norm. The failure to sense the categorical difference between individual behaviour in the market and in voting stems presumably from an unexamined transference of the economists' bare-bones definition of subjective utility to the setting where more than ordinality is required to explain behaviour. In collective interaction, the outcome finally selected emerges from the inputs of all participants, as these are aggregated through some process, some institutional framework, some decision rule or rules. Each and every participant recognizes that his input, his vote, will not determine the outcome. But, at the same time, each and every participant knows that his vote, at least probabilistically, will affect the outcome.

In this sense, any vote must be 'strategic' if this term is used to imply that any change in the behaviour of the single voter can modify the outcome that emerges. There can be no voting behaviour that is 'nonstrategic'. Mathematically, it is useful to think of the outcome of a voting process as a vector, with the separate inputs as components. Change in any input will change the position of the vector. Confusion arises here because, under normal settings, the alternatives are discrete and limited in number. The change in the behaviour of a single voter may, in many instances, leave the observed collective outcome unchanged. Probabilistically, however, and in an *ex ante* sense, a change in any vote can affect the emergent outcome. And this result holds regardless of the size of the voting group.

The term 'strategic voting' should be limited to those small-number settings in which the change in the behaviour of one participant may modify the outcome *through changing the behaviour of other participants*. This prospect disappears in large-number settings, in which the individual takes the behaviour of others to be beyond his direct control. An acknowledged inability to control the voting behaviour of others through changes in the single voter's own behaviour does not, however, imply an inability to predict the patterns of such behaviour and to use these predictions in voting choice.

CONCLUSION

Our purpose in this chapter is limited. The argument is aimed to sever the relationship between the individual's primitive ordering over the set of potential outcomes for the collectivity – the set from which some 'political choice' is to be made – and the ordering of the individual's choices as revealed in voting behaviour. The categorical distinction between these two orderings has not been directly recognized in conventional analyses, and voting behaviour that exhibits departure from the primitive ordering has been presumed to be the focus of further inquiry. More explicit recognition of the distinction here should send many public choice analysts 'back to the drawing board', especially if their ultimate objective is to explain observed behaviour in politics, as opposed to derivation of a 'social' scalar.

Note that we do not go beyond attention to the decision calculus of the individual as one among a set of participants in collective action. We make no effort to examine the implications of the analysis here to an understanding and explanation of how the voting choices of individuals are aggregated to generate a collective result. There is no direct linkage to the continuing Arrow puzzle that involves efforts to derive a rational social ordering from individual preferences, whether these be treated as primitive or as revealed in voting behaviour.

Our initial intent was to examine the implications of the analysis for the stability of majoritarian political processes. Does the incorporation of the individual voter's ability to evaluate alternatives subjectively, over and beyond the base ordinal ranking presumed in conventional analysis, possibly supply a partial answer to Gordon Tullock's question: Why so much stability? (Tullock, 1981). Our preliminary inquiry suggests that this question requires analysis that is well beyond the scope of this chapter.

NOTES

1. Several theorists have attempted to extend the primitive preference ordering to allow for 'strategic' departures from such linkage, while adhering to precepts of rational behaviour. (See, for example, Farquharson, 1969; Gibbard, 1973; Satterthwaite, 1975.) Such efforts seem misguided in their failure to appreciate that the distinctive setting within which choices are made eliminates the relevance of any primitive ordering of end-states. Austen-Smith and Banks (1998, 2000) recognize the categorical distinction here, but from a perspective different from our own.
2. The distinction examined in this section was analysed in an early paper by Buchanan (1954b).
3. This point was central to Buchanan's 1954 critique of Arrow (Buchanan, 1954a).
4. In one interpretation, this becomes Arrow's requirement of the independence of irrelevant alternatives. If the voter does not know that other than the two alternatives confronted are in existence, it is clear that rationality cannot dictate departure from the primitive ordering, which then becomes possible only if this condition is violated.
5. Let r be defined by $r = [U(B) - U(C)]/[U(A) - U(B)]$. Voter 1 will vote contrary to his primitive ordering if benefits exceed costs, if $\{U(B) - [U(A) + U(B) + U(C)]/3\} > 2[U(A) - U(B)]$. By forcing equality and substituting $[U(B) - U(C)] = r[U(A) - U(B)]$ in the equality relation, we obtain the critical value, $r = 7$, in this specified informational setting.

REFERENCES

Arrow, Kenneth (1951), *Social Choice and Individual Values*, New York: Wiley.

Austen-Smith, David and Jeffrey S. Banks (1998), 'Social Choice Theory, Game Theory, and Positive Political Economy', in N. Polsby (ed.), *Annual Review of Political Science*, vol. 1, Palo Alto: Annual Reviews, pp. 259–87.

Austen-Smith, David and Jeffrey S. Banks (2000), *Positive Political Theory I: Collective Preference*, Ann Arbor: University of Michigan Press.

Buchanan, James M. (1954a), 'Social Choice, Democracy, and Free Markets', *Journal of Political Economy*, **62** (April), 114–23.

Buchanan, James M. (1954b), 'Individual Choice in Voting and the Market', *Journal of Political Economy*, **62** (August), 334–43.

Farquharson, Robin (1969), *Theory of Voting*, New Haven: Yale University Press.

Gibbard, Allan (1973), 'Manipulation of Voting Schemes: A General Result', *Econometrica*, **41** (July), 587–602.

Robbins, Lionel (1932), *The Nature and Significance of Economic Science*, London: Macmillan.

Satterthwaite, Mark A. (1975), 'Strategy-Proofness and Arrow's Conditions: Existence and Correspondence Theorems for Voting Procedures and Social Welfare Functions', *Journal of Political Economy*, **10** (April), 187–217.

Sen, Amartya (1995), 'Rationality and Social Choice', *American Economic Review*, **85** (1, March), 1–24.

Tullock, Gordon (1981), 'Why So Much Stability?' *Public Choice*, **37**, 189–202.

APPENDIX 5A

Voting Choice Under Total Ignorance of Voting Patterns of Others

Imagine a person in total ignorance of other voters' preferences or voting orders. Such a person may vote according to his primitive ordinal preferences. We analyse this conjecture in pairwise majority voting.

Consider the voting model for three persons and three alternatives. The alternatives, A, B and C, are exogenously given. Among the three voters, 1, 2 and 3, we consider voter 1 as the reference voter and analyse his voting behaviour. Without loss of generality, we assume that the reference voter's ordinal preference is (ABC); A is preferred to B which is preferred to C. There are six possible voting orders represented by letters x, x^*, y, y^*, z and z^*:

x	x^*	y	y^*	z	z^*
A	A	B	B	C	C
B	C	C	A	A	B
C	B	A	C	B	A

We apply the Laplace hypothesis and assume that the reference voter assigns equal probability, one-sixth, to each of the six possible voting orders listed. The reference voter may act on the basis of any one of the alternative voting orders x^*, y, y^*, z and z^* with only the first, x, reflecting this primitive preference ordering.

To identify a dominant voting order for the reference voter, we compare the voting outcome of each voting order in each category. We first calculate the voting outcome when the reference voter acts on the basis of his primitive preference order, $x = (ABC)$.

There are 36 possible voting combinations for the pair of voters 2 and 3. These 36 combinations can be classified into the three categories below.

Category 1
There are 12 cases in this category with voters 2 and 3 having identical highest-ranked alternatives. The voting outcome for each case is shown below:

	Voting outcome
xxx, xxx^*, xx^*x, xx^*x^*:	A
xyy, xyy^*, xy^*y, xy^*y^*:	B
xzz, xzz^*, xz^*z, xz^*z^*:	C

Voting outcomes in this category are stable and are beyond the influence of the reference voter.

Category 2
Either one, but not both, of voters 2 or 3 has A as the highest-ranked alternative. There are 16 possible cases listed below:

	Voting outcome
xx $(y, y^*, z$ or $z^*)$:	A
x $(y, y^*, z$ or $z^*)$ x:	A
xx^* $(y, y^*$ z or $z^*)$:	A
x $(y, y^*, z$ or $z^*)$ x^*:	A

The voting outcome is A for each case in this category. The reference voter can influence the outcome, but he has no incentive to deviate from his primitive ordinal ranking because A is his highest-ranked alternative.

Category 3
Each of the three persons has a different highest-ranked alternative. There are eight cases which, together with entries in categories 1 and 2, exhaust the 36 total possible cases. The voting outcomes are:

Table 5A.1

	Voting outcome
(i) xyz and xzy:	cycle
(ii) xyz^* and xz^*y:	B
(iii) xy^*z and xzy^*:	A
(iv) xy^*z^* and xz^*y^*:	B

The next step is to calculate the voting outcome when the reference voter adopts a voting order that differs from his primitive preference order. First, consider $x^* = (ACB)$. Note that A remains the highest-ranked alternative.

Voting outcomes in categories 1 and 2 do not change. But category 3 gives different outcomes as shown in Table 5A.2:

We compare the outcomes of the two voting orders x and x^* adopted by the reference voter. From Tables 5A.1 and 5A.2, we note that voting order x generates 'one A, two Bs and one cycle', while voting order x^* generates 'one A, two Cs and one cycle'. Thus,

Result 1:   For the reference voter, voting order x dominates voting order x^*.

Table 5A.2

		Voting outcome
(v)	x^*yz and x^*zy:	C
(vi)	x^*yz^* and x^*z^*y:	C
(vii)	x^*y^*z and x^*zy^*:	A
(viii)	$x^*y^*z^*$ and $x^*z^*y^*$:	cycle

It is trivial to show that voting order x for the reference voter dominates voting orders $z = (CAB)$ and $z^* = (CBA)$.

Now suppose that the reference voter considers voting orders y and y^*. By comparing the outcomes of y and y^*, we show that y^* dominates y. In conclusion, we compare voting orders x and y^*.

First, suppose that the reference voter adopts voting order $y = (BCA)$. For category 1, his vote has no influence. For category 3, the outcome is B for each case. The cases in category 2 are analysed below.

For the following eight cases in category 2, the outcome is B:

	Voting outcome
yxy, yxy^*, yyx, yy^*x:	B
yx^*y, yx^*y^*, yyx^*, yy^*x^*:	B

The voting outcomes for the remaining eight cases from category 2 are:

Table 5A.3

	Voting outcome
yxz, yzx:	cycle
yxz^*, yz^*x:	B
yx^*z, yzx^*:	C
yx^*z^*, yz^*x^*:	C

Suppose the reference voter adopts $y^* = (BAC)$, the outcomes are the same as y for categories 1, 3 and the first eight cases in category 2. Voting outcomes for the remaining eight cases from category 2 are:
The outcome of y^* is 'one A, two Bs and one cycle' which dominates the outcome from y. Thus,

Result 2:   The reference voter is better off by adopting voting order y^* rather than y.

Table 5A.4

	Voting outcome
y^*xz, y^*zx:	A
y^*xz^*, y^*z^*x:	B
y^*x^*z, y^*zx^*:	B
$y^*x^*z^*, y^*z^*x^*$:	cycle

With these two results we are now ready to prove our conjecture that the voter in total ignorance will vote primitively.

Proposition: If a person has to vote under total ignorance, he will vote according to his primitive preference ordering.

Proof: From Results 1 and 2, it will suffice to show that, for the reference voter, the outcome of voting primitively dominates the outcome of voting order y^*. We compare the outcomes for voting orders x and y^* below.

For category 1, the outcomes of x and y^* are the same. For category 2, for the first eight cases, y^* generates the outcomes

	Voting outcome
$y^*xy, y^*xy^*, y^*yx, y^*y^*x$:	B (A)
$y^*x^*y, y^*x^*y^*, y^*yx^*, y^*y^*x^*$:	B (A)

where the letter in parenthesis is the outcome of voting order x. For the remaining eight cases from category 2, from Table 5A.4

	Voting outcome	
y^*xz, y^*:	A	(A)
y^*xz^*, y^*z^*x:	B	(A)
y^*x^*z, y^*zx^*:	B	(A)
$y^*x^*z^*, y^*z^*x^*$:	cycle	(A)

For category 3, the outcome of voting order y^* is B for each case,

	Voting outcome	
(i) xyz and xzy:	B	(cycle)
(ii) xyz^* and xz^*y:	B	(B)
(iii) xy^*z and xzy^*:	B	(A)
(iv) xy^*z^* and xz^*y^*:	B	(B)

where letters in parenthesis are the outcomes of voting order x. (See Table 5A.1.)

Consider the cycle case in category 3(i) above. The reference voter plays y^*, and the voting outcome is B instead of a cycle. But note that voting order y^* also creates a cycle in category 2 at the expense of outcome A. The net result is equivalent to getting outcome B at the expense of outcome A. Thus, the primitive voting order, x, dominates the voting order y^*. This proves that the voter in total ignorance has no incentive to vote other than according to his primitive preferences.

Q.E.D.

Note.   This proposition suggests that the voter may deviate from his primitive preference order only when he has some knowledge of the voting order of other voters. Also, note that the proof is based purely on ordinal rankings; there is no need to introduce subjective evaluation of alternatives.

6.   Truth, justice and democracy*

Robert E. Goodin[†]

Geoff Brennan is an uncharacteristic economist in a great many ways. Not least among them is his ongoing engagement with philosophy on the one side and politics on the other – uniting in his penetrating explorations of the justificatory logic of democratic rule.[1] Here I hope to further that project by exploring the ways in which democracy might be an aid in pursuing both truth and justice.

There are many different conceptions of both 'truth' and 'justice'. I shall not say anything much here about those controversies. Basically, I shall just be relying on a commonsensical notion of truth, stripped of any philosophical complications. And among the many theories of justice on offer, I shall just be relying on the one that equates justice with impartial want-satisfaction.

Many grounds have been offered, over the years, for thinking that democracy promotes both truth and justice. I canvass several of them briefly. But my principal aim here is to analyse two closely related arguments that admit of parallel mathematical formulations. One is the Condorcet Jury Theorem, showing that the outcome of a majority vote among a large number of independent and modestly competent voters on an issue of fact will almost certainly be the correct outcome. The other is the Majority Rule Theorem, showing that simple majority rule is the decision rule which best promotes impartial justice, analysed in terms of the expectations of a voter with uncertain preferences ending up on the winning side in an election.[2]

In combining those two models in the ways I do here, my fundamental motivational assumption is that people want social decision procedures that track the truth in matters of fact and that track their preferences in matters purely of preference. Of course, people may have preferences over matters of fact – they wish that certain things were true, and that others were not. But such 'wishful thinking' is a cognitive defect to which people seeking to satisfy their preferences dare not succumb (Elster, 1983, ch. 4). Wishfully mistaking facts interferes with the identification of the optimal course of action for satisfying one's (other) preferences.[3] Preference-satisfiers seeking optimal ways of satisfying their preferences thus ought rationally to maximize truth-satisfaction first.

Both the Condorcet Jury Theorem and the Majority Rule Theorem depend on various assumptions. One assumption (which I shall continue making here) is that people represent their beliefs and their preferences sincerely in the way they vote, rather than strategically misrepresenting them in the hope of manipulating the outcome. Another assumption that both those theorems require is statistical independence among all the voters. That assumption will here be relaxed.

The assumption that voters are all statistically independent of one another corresponds tolerably well to the conditions in certain sorts of societies. And where it does – in radically individualistic societies of independent voters – the theorems linking democracy to truth and justice both hold firm. Other societies, however, are quite unlike that. Under conditions of 'social unity' and conformist voting, these twin theorems would lead us to expect that democracy yields outcomes that are less reliably truthful but more reliably just. Under conditions of radical social segmentation of opposing groups, similar logic ought to lead us to expect democracy's performance might be worse in both dimensions. Democratic rule by simple majorities may still be better than any alternative, even in seriously divided societies. It is simply the case that, there, democracy delivers both less truth and less justice.

HOW DEMOCRACY CAN SERVE TRUTH

It is a familiar proposition that democratic institutions can aid in the pursuit of the truth. Just recall the discussion of free speech in John Stuart Mill's essay *On Liberty*.[4] Truth, Mill supposes, will inevitably win out in the competition of ideas which democracy encourages, and which freedom of discussion (which is part and parcel of democracy) makes possible. That was conventional wisdom, even in Mill's own day. 'Let [Truth] and Falsehood grapple; who ever knew Truth put to the worse in a free and open encounter?', John Milton had asked rhetorically, fully two centuries before.[5]

Today's corresponding catchphrase dubs democracy a 'marketplace of ideas' in which, once again, truth necessary prevails. The phrase was itself coined by that most famous American judge, Oliver Wendell Holmes, and has won the endorsement of at least one Nobel Laureate in Economics.[6] Despite that pedigree, I am unpersuaded. It may well be that the truth prevails in open discussions – but if so, that is not because the public forum is like an economic market.[7]

Economists provide elegant mathematical proofs that competition in free markets maximizes human happiness (at least in the sense of 'guaranteeing Pareto optimality'). But those proofs presuppose lots of things about the nature of the goods and the nature of the competition. Those presuppositions often prove untrue even of the commodities that are literally bought and sold in ordinary economic markets. They are all the more untrue of 'ideas' that are supposed to be 'bought' and 'sold' in the metaphorical 'marketplace of ideas'.

For example, markets presuppose well defined property rights: you can sell something, and in that way transfer a property title in it to someone else, only if you own the title in the first place. Markets presuppose that property is transferred, from buyer to seller. And markets presuppose that actors are always trying to 'buy cheap and sell dear'. But typically no one 'owns' ideas, as such.[8] When you 'sell' someone else your idea, you do not lose it; the other simply comes to share it. And when the other 'buys' your idea, he gives you nothing (except psychic gratification, perhaps) in exchange for it and he sacrifices nothing (except error) in acquiring it. In short, 'ideas' are just not marketable goods, in any important sense.

Even if they were, the logic of market competition gives us no reason to suppose that the ideas that prevail there will be true ideas, as opposed to merely 'appealing' or 'comforting' ones. There are certain things that we would *like* to believe. All that the economic proofs say is that free competition in perfectly functioning markets gives people what they want, to the greatest extent possible. If people prefer comforting fictions to hard truths, that is what free market competition in ideas will give them. (Of course, if that is what people want – and if 'happiness' equates to want-satisfaction – then that might be a good way of maximizing human happiness. But I take it that the virtue of hard truths is not just that they are 'hard' but that they are *true*, and that acting on true beliefs will – as a general rule, anyway – help us get more of the other things we want. In the short term, some happiness might be sacrificed by denying people their comforting fictions. But in the longer term more happiness will ordinarily be gained by facing up to hard truths. Or so I presume here.)

A more persuasive case for thinking that democracy promotes truth is to be found in models of information-pooling. Those, like so much else, can be traced back to Aristotle.[9] His own claim about the 'wisdom of the multitude' was simple: alone, I know A; alone, you know B; but when we pool our knowledge, we each come to know both A and B.

In that simplest form, of course, the argument will not quite work. Implicit in that simple argument is the further claim, analogous to the central proposition which I have just criticized about the 'marketplace of ideas', that good ideas drive out bad. What Aristotle is implicitly counting on is that, when you and I come together, you will embrace my truth and I yours. The opposite might equally well occur, however. Bad ideas might drive out good. When you and I come together, instead of embracing each

other's truths (*A* and *B*) we might end up embracing each other's follies
(both coming to believe not-*A* and not-*B*). What matters is not *that* we pool
but rather *what* we filter into the pool.

The Condorcet Jury Theorem: an Informal Presentation

The best argument for thinking that democracy promotes the truth builds
on that idea of information-pooling, but in a very different way. This is the
famous Condorcet Jury Theorem, first published in 1785 but not resur-
rected and properly integrated into mainstream democratic theory until
two centuries later.[10]

Technical details are provided below. But basically the Condorcet Jury
Theorem works through the 'law of large numbers'. Suppose that the probability of something happening is *p*. It could be anything: a coin coming
up 'heads' when you flip it; my guessing, purely by chance, the right answer
on a multiple choice test; our next child being a girl; whatever. On any
given occasion, the outcome will be all one thing or all the other. And even
if we repeat the process a few times, it would not be all that surprising if
three tosses of a fair coin all came up heads. But suppose we repeat the
process many times (flip the coin twenty times, guess on twenty test questions, have twenty more kids); and suppose, furthermore, that each of these
successive trials is independent of the others. Then statistically we ought
to expect the frequency with which outcomes emerge to be pretty close to
the *ex ante* probability (*p*) of their occurring. And the more times we
repeat the process, the closer the observed frequency ought be to the probability for each outcome. If the probability of a tossed coin coming up
heads is 50 percent, then the outcome of lots of flips ought to be 50 percent
heads.

That much is just 'Statistics I'. Here is how the Condorcet Jury Theorem
adapts those standard propositions to bear on democratic politics. Suppose
that the outcome in question is 'voting for a true proposition'. (It is easiest
to think of all this in connection with literal juries, where the defendant
truly is either innocent or guilty.) Suppose that the probability of each
person voting for a true proposition is *p*. Finally, suppose that each person's
vote is independent of every other person's vote. Just as a very few coin-flips
might produce an odd pattern of results, so too might a vote among a small
number of people. But now let the number of voters grow large. Then by
the same 'law of large numbers' as before, the observed frequency of outcomes (here, voting for a true proposition) ought be pretty close to the
probability *p* of each voter voting for a true proposition. If the probability
of each of us voting correctly was 60 percent, then the true proposition
should in a large electorate win 60 percent of the votes.

Now, of course, in a democratic election what matters is not so much the margin of victory as the fact of victory – being the first past the post. The same mathematics underlying the previous result can be used to calculate the overall 'probability of the truth winning'. This is where the Condorcet Jury Theorem results become really compelling. Suppose, for example, that the probability of each voter voting correctly is just 51 percent. Then the probability that the correct outcome will be supported by a majority of 1000 such voters is 69 percent; and the probability of its being supported by a majority of 10 000 such voters is 99.97 percent.[11]

Impressive numbers they may be. But there is no magic involved. It is just the 'law of large numbers' again. The more independent trials there are (here, the more people there are independently casting their votes), the more likely it is that the observed frequency (here, of correct votes) will match the probability of each independent trial turning out that way (here, each of us voting correctly). Just so long as each of us is more than half-likely to be right, the probability that a large group of us will be wrong is vanishingly small.

For expository convenience, I have so far been talking of the simplest case – the case of majority voting among just two propositions, where every voter has exactly the same probability of voting correctly. Be assured, however, that the Condorcet Jury Theorem works perfectly well in a range of other circumstances as well. Thus, for example, we can let the probability of voters voting correctly vary across voters; the Condorcet theorem still holds, just so long as those varying probabilities are symmetrical around the mean and the mean probability is above 0.5. Or, again, we can let the vote be among more than two alternatives; again, the Condorcet theorem still holds. Indeed, it holds all the more strongly if we stick to the demand that an alternative must get more than half the votes to win. But the theorem also holds for plurality voting over k options, just so long as probability of each voter voting correctly (or the mean probability, among voters with symmetrically distributed probabilities) is greater than $1/k$.[12] Sample calculations suggest that broadly the same is true for any of the most standardly employed social decision procedures (run-off elections, pairwise votes, the Borda count and so on).[13] The bottom line really does seem to be that, provided the average voter is more likely to be right than random, the outcome of a democratic procedure is almost certain to track the truth in a large electorate.

There are three main things that might limit the applicability of that result to real-world politics. One is that that argument works only where there is some 'truth of the matter' for voting to track. In a jury voting on the guilt or innocence of a defendant, there might be; in many of the things put to a democratic vote, there might not be.[14] A second is that the

Condorcet Jury Theorem really does presuppose that voters are, on average, more likely to be right than wrong.[15] If voters are more likely to be wrong than right, then the 'law of large numbers' works as powerfully in the opposite direction and the larger the electorate is the more certain it is of coming to the wrong conclusion. Third and finally, the Condorcet Jury Theorem presupposes that each person's vote is statistically independent of each other person's.

Ponder that last limitation for a moment. Imagine a shareholder's meeting where there are just ten real people physically present, but where each of them holds proxy votes for 10 000 other shareholders. The effective size of that electorate, for purposes of Condorcet Jury Theorem calculations, is ten rather than 100 000. The reason is simply that the votes of all 10 000 of his proxies are fully determined by whichever way their nominated representative decides to vote. There are only ten degrees of freedom here, not 100 000.

The need for statistical independence among voters to make the Condorcet Jury Theorem work is something about which I say more later. Let me just flag that as an 'interesting problem'. The other two potential threats seem to me only mildly threatening, though. Truth is rarely all that there is to political disputes. But most political disputes concern what are true facts of the matter, at least in part. And while we may not have a very high estimation of our fellow citizens' competence, I doubt that many of us would really want to insist that they were systematically worse than 'random' across the range of things on which their political opinions might be sought.

In short, I think that the sort of information-pooling model represented by the Condorcet Jury Theorem pretty persuasively demonstrates that democracy is a good truth-tracker. If there are truths to be found, a democratic vote among a large electorate is highly likely to find them.

More Formally

These informal remarks can be formalized in the following terms:

Calculating the probability of an option winning
The probability $P_\emptyset$ of a option $\emptyset$ winning a majority of at least w out of N total votes, each of which is statistically independent of every other, is

$$P_\emptyset = \sum_{i=w}^{N} (N!/[N-i]!i!)\, (p)^i (1-p)^{N-i} \tag{6.1}$$

where p is the probability of a voter (which is assumed to be the same for all voters)[16] will vote for option $\emptyset$, in a two-option contest. In talking about majority requirement, I will use w as in equation (6. 1) to denote the absolute number of votes required to win and m to denote the proportion of total votes required to win ($m = w/N$).

Calculating the probability of the truth winning

For purposes of the Condorcet Jury Theorem, ø is taken to be the 'correct' option, p as representing the probability that each voter will vote for that option, and $P_ø$ is the probability that the correct option ø will win by securing a majority of m of the votes.

The Condorcet Jury Theorem states for the two-option case that, if $p > 0.5$, then $P_ø$ is an increasing function of N and tends toward one as N approaches infinity. By the same logic, if $p < 0.5$, then $P_ø$ is a decreasing function of N and tends toward zero as N approaches infinity.

For $0.5 < p < 1$, sample calculations reveal that values of $P_ø$ near to one can be obtained with modest-sized Ns (10 to 20, for example) if p is high (0.8 or so); but where p is only barely over 0.5 it takes larger Ns (in the thousands) to achieve values of $P_ø$ very near to one. Where N is very large (hundreds of thousands or more), however, $P_ø$ is arbitrarily near to one for virtually any value of $p > 0.5$.

HOW DEMOCRACY CAN SERVE JUSTICE

Democracy, it is standardly said, has procedural as well as epistemic virtues. Besides helping us to find the truth, democracy also helps us to promote justice.[17]

At its narrowest, that might be read just as a boast about formal properties of democratic procedures themselves. Looking at politics as a 'game', we might suppose that the various procedural safeguards associated with democratic rule ensure 'fair play'. Sometimes those intuitions about fairness are left as relatively unanalysed pre-analytic givens. Other times they are tied back to, and justified in terms of, some deeper moral values, like freedom, equality and the dignity of the individual.[18]

Alternatively, democratic procedures might be said to promote justice of a substantive, not 'purely procedural', sort. That claim would be an empty tautology, however, if democracy were defined as just part of what justice requires, or if justice were defined as just whatever outcomes were democratically chosen. For that to be an interesting claim rather than a mere tautology, we thus need some independent specification both of what counts as democracy and what counts as justice.

The Majority Rule Theorem: an Informal Statement

Here I want to explore one particular version of that sort of argument, the one most directly connected to the claim that democracy maximizes impartial want-satisfaction. This is a line of thought historically associated with another Mill (1823) – James, father of John Stuart and disciple of Jeremy Bentham. That proposition has been developed in many different ways by many different authors, over the years. Here I want to focus the one that is structurally most similar to the Condorcet Jury Theorem, just discussed.

The basic trick in this argument is essentially the same as Rawls's (1971) 'veil of ignorance'. Suppose you are having to choose 'basic institutions' for your society, in the absence of any detailed knowledge of how they are going to impact on you in particular. In Rawls's version of the story, we are supposed to 'forget' (for the purposes of making this choice in a morally appropriate manner) things that we actually know about our preferences and social situations. But there is no need to engage in that philosophical fantasy, here. Genuine uncertainty can sometimes come close to performing the same trick (Harsanyi, 1953, 1982). Whatever basic institutions we put into place are likely to last a long time; we have no good way of knowing how our preferences and social situations might vary over so long a time; and therefore we have no good way of knowing with any confidence exactly how well or badly any particular arrangements would serve our shifting interests.

In terms of theories of justice, the great virtue of 'veils of ignorance' or their uncertainty equivalents is that they force people to choose impartially. Even if you are only trying to maximize your own want-satisfaction, the uncertainty associated with long-term institutional choices means that you do not know what your own particular circumstances will be (what you will want or what will best deliver it to you). To maximize the chances that your own future wants will be satisfied, therefore, you have no alternative except to try to maximize the satisfaction of everyone's future wants overall. Not knowing which social position you will occupy, maximizing most people's well-being gives you the best chance of maximizing your own long-term well-being (Harsanyi, 1982; see similarly Edgeworth, 1925, pp. 102–3; Hicks, 1941, p. 111; and Goodin, 1976, pp. 76–80).

That is a familiar philosophical move within the theory of justice. Notice now, however, that the same basic model can be adapted to serve as a defence of democracy. In the case of distributive justice, the basic idea was that if you didn't know who you would turn out to be then the best way to make sure you will turn out to have a good income was to maximize the proportion of the population that has a good income. The larger the percentage of the population that is in a favourable position, the better your chances of randomly being among those in a favourable position. In the case of politics, the same is true. If you don't know which side of future issues you will be on, the best way of ensuring that you will turn out to be on the winning side is to maximize the proportion of the population who on the winning side. The larger the percentage of the population that is in is on the winning side, the better your chances of randomly being among them.

On the face of it, that might look like an argument for a unanimity rule. If nothing can be enacted without everyone's consent, then everyone is on the winning side of every successful proposition (Buchanan and Tullock, 1962; Brennan and Buchanan, 1980). But it is equally true, under a unanimity rule, that *almost* everyone can turn out to be on the losing side of every unsuccessful proposition. Under a unanimity rule, every person has a veto that can be used to frustrate the wishes of everyone else, however large their majority (Rae, 1975).

In calculating the probability of being on the winning side, therefore, we have to be 'case sensitive'. That is to say, we have to take account both of the probability of a proposition winning if you want it to win and of the probability of a proposition not winning if you want it not to win.

Simple majority rule has been proven to be the decision rule that uniquely maximizes that probability (Rae, 1969; Taylor, 1969; cf. Straffin, 1977). Henceforth, therefore, I refer to this line of argument as the Majority Rule Theorem. The proof works through a logic parallel to the Condorcet Jury Theorem, as demonstrated below. That existing result pertains to only one particular version of 'symmetrical' special majority rules. Below I extend the argument to 'asymmetrical special majority rules' as well.

Here again, then, we have a formal proof that democracy maximizes impartial want-satisfaction, and justice in that sense. But here again, I should emphasize that that proof formally depends on the assumption that everyone's vote is statistically independent of everyone else's. Later I turn to consider what happens when people's votes are interlinked.

Calculating the Probability of Each Voter's Winning

In the case of the Majority Rule Theorem, p in equation (6.1) is taken to represent the probability that each voter will vote for option ø, and $1 - p$ as the probability that each voter will vote for option not-ø. (We assume for convenience that no voter abstains.) As before, $P_ø$ represents the probability that option ø will win and $P_{not-ø}$ the probability that option not-ø will win.

To reckon the probability of any given voter being on the winning side, we need to consider two possibilities. One is that he will vote for option ø, with probability p. The other is that he will vote for option not-ø, with probability $1 - p$. As N approaches infinity, the probability P_w that any given voter will be on the winning side approaches:

$$P_w = pP_\emptyset + (1 - p)(P_{\text{not-}\emptyset}) \tag{6.2}$$

Consider first the standard case: in a two-option case, either one option or the other is chosen as the social outcome (so $P_\emptyset = 1 - P_{\text{not-}\emptyset}$). As N approaches infinity, $P_\emptyset$ approaches one if $p > m$ and zero if $p < m$. It therefore follows from equation (6.2) that, as N approaches infinity, Pw approaches p where $p > m$ and $(1 - p)$ where $(1 - p) > m$.

For simple majority rule ($m = 0.5$) that virtually exhausts all the possible outcomes. The only remaining case is where $p = (1 - p) = m = 0.5$, in which case P_w also equals 0.5. For special majority rules where $m > 0.5$, however, there can be other cases that need to be considered.

Social decision rules that set $m > 0.5$ are called, generically, 'special majority rules'. These can take either of two more specific forms.[19] The 'symmetrical' form is what is presupposed in the standard Majority Rule Theorem. There, any option has to achieve the same special majority (m) of votes in order to be established as the social choice; if no option gets m or more votes, then none is socially chosen. With symmetrical special majority rules, then, it can happen that $P_\emptyset$ and $P_{\text{not-}\emptyset}$ sum to less than one.

With the 'asymmetrical' special majority rules, one option is established as the 'default option'. That option is then the social choice unless some other option gets m or more votes (which is consistent with the 'default' option itself receiving less than m votes). In the case of asymmetrical special majority rules, therefore, it is always the case that $P_{\text{not-}\emptyset} = (1 - P_\emptyset)$.

The great disadvantage of the 'symmetrical' version is that it leaves some issues unresolved. The great disadvantage of the 'asymmetrical' version is that it contains a bias in favour of some option (whichever is identified as the 'default') over others (Goodin and List, 2005). Both those features are unwelcome from the point of view of justice, understood as maximum impartial want-satisfaction.

To apply that standard of 'impartial want-satisfaction', imagine someone concerned with his probability of winning over a range of uncertain future votes. When symmetrical special majority rules prove indeterminate, choosing no outcome as the winner, the absolute probability P_w of that voter's preferred outcome winning is correspondingly reduced. Thus, symmetrical special majority rules fail the 'maximize want-satisfaction' portion of our desideratum of 'maximizing impartial want-satisfaction'.

Consider next asymmetrical special majority rules. Those introduce a bias in favour of a default option, relative to other options. That bias, in turn, imposes a risk (the greater the bias, the greater the risk) on a voter whose preferences are uncertain over a range of future options: he does not know whether his preferred option will turn out to be the default option or not. Someone concerned with his probability of winning will presumably be anxious both to maximize his probabilistic expectation of winning and also to minimize risk. And what appears intrapersonally as 'risk' appears interpersonally as a violation of impartiality. The more a decision procedure is biased toward one outcome or toward one voter (or group of voters), the more that procedure fails the standard of 'impartiality'.[20] Asymmetrical special majority rules thus fail the 'impartiality' portion of our desideratum of 'maximizing impartial want-satisfaction'.

Focusing first on issues of 'maximizing want-satisfaction', there is reason to think that an asymmetrical special majority rule always yields a higher probability of winning (P_w) than does a symmetrical special majority rule employing the same m. Suppose not-ø is the default option that 'wins' if neither option attains the requisite m votes. If the uncertain voter turns out to want not-ø his probability of getting what he wants is greater under the asymmetrical rule than the symmetrical rule; whereas if the voter turns out to want ø his probability of getting what he wants is exactly the same under both asymmetrical and symmetrical rules employing the same m.

While asymmetrical special majority rules are always in that respect preferred to symmetrical ones, further reflection on the preferred value of m suggests that a simple majority rule ($m = 0.5$) is always preferable to special majority rules ($m > 0.5$) of either sort.

Under symmetrical special majority rules, increasing values of m (the size of the 'special majority' that is required) are associated with increasing numbers of 'no decisions' and, hence, with decreasing values of P_w. To maximize P_w symmetrical majority rules need to minimize m, with $m = 0.5$ being the smallest value of m that is consistent with a social decision rule's being decisive at all in a two-option case. (Multiple incompatible options might simultaneously be socially chosen if $m < 0.5$[21]).

Under asymmetrical special majority rules, increasing values of m are associated with increasing bias in favour of the default option. That leads to increasing risk from the point of view of voters uncertain as to which option they will prefer in a range of future choices. To minimize the risk – which is to say, to minimize the difference between the probability of winning if you favour an option and the probability of winning if you oppose it – asymmetrical majority rules need once again to minimize m. Once again, in the two-option case $m = 0.5$ is the minimum value for a decisive social decision rule in the two-option case. And recall again that what appears intrapersonally as risk appears interpersonally as a failure of impartiality. So to maximize impartiality as well as to minimize risk, $m = 0.5$ is the preferred value of m under asymmetrical majority rule.

For those different but related reasons, both symmetrical and asymmetrical decision rules should therefore set for the two-option case at $m = 0.5$ (or for the more general k-option case at $m = (1/k)$). That is to say, of course, that the decision rule should not be special majority rule but, rather, simple majority rule.

Even for simple majority rule, there can still be a difference between symmetrical and asymmetrical versions of that rule. The difference arises in the case of a literally tied vote. Symmetrical simple-majority rules yield no decision in a tie, whereas asymmetrical simple-majority rules decide in favour of the default option. Hence, as before, the probability of winning P_w is therefore always slightly higher for the asymmetrical version of simple majority rule. But the difference is virtually immaterial in a large electorate. (As N approaches infinity, the probability of exactly the same number of votes for both ø and not-ø approaches zero, and P_w with an asymmetrical rule setting $m = 0.5$ approaches P_w with a symmetrical rule setting $m = 0.5$.)

UNITY: SOCIAL CONFORMISM

Both of those standard results – connecting democracy to truth (through the Condorcet Jury Theorem) and to justice (through the Majority Rule Theorem) – presuppose individualism of a fairly strong sort. Specifically, they presuppose that each person's vote is statistically completely independent of each other person's vote.

Now let us reflect on what happens to those results, firstly under the opposite assumption of absolute unity (conformity) across the community, and then (in the next section) under conditions of 'unity and diversity' (clusters of unified groups: a segmented society). To foreshadow, it turns out that society-wide unity makes democracy more just but less truthful, whereas clustering might (depending on its details) undermine democracy's performance in both respects.

Complete Societal Conformism: Perfect Positive Interconnection

Consider first the case of absolute unity society-wide. There, everyone thinks the same thing as everyone else; everyone votes the same way as everyone else. Furthermore, they do so out of motives of sheer conformism. They think that way, and vote that way, *because* that is how everyone else thinks and votes – that, instead of having independently come to the same conclusions for themselves.[22]

In this case of perfect positive interconnection, the way in which one person votes completely (and positively) determines the way in which every other person votes. If one person votes ø, then everyone else will also vote ø. If one person votes not-ø then everyone else will vote not-ø.

In those circumstances, the truth-tracking power of democracy is lost. However many actual voters there may be, you have effectively only one distinct point of view represented. It is like the example of the shareholder meeting discussed earlier – except here it is as if a single person held everyone's proxy. The probability that that election produces the 'correct' outcome is simply the probability that that single individual has of selecting the correct outcome; no more.

The justice-tracking power of democracy is, however, greatly enhanced in such circumstances of absolute unity. If everyone votes the same way as everyone else, then everyone is guaranteed always to be on the winning side in every election. If one person votes ø, then everyone else will also, and option ø is certain to win; if one person votes not-ø then everyone votes not-ø and option not-ø is certain to win. No one wants to see something enacted that does not get enacted. No one wants to see some proposal stopped that is not stopped.

In this limiting case of perfect positive interconnection, of course, that is equally true of any decision rule that is broadly democratic, in the sense of being 'positively responsive to people's preferences'. With *perfect* positive interconnection among people's preferences, there is literally no difference between simple majority rule, special majority rules or any of myriad other positively-responsive decision procedures. Similarly, in the limiting case of *perfect* positive interconnection, it might seem odd to talk about 'maximizing impartial want-satisfaction' (it is impossible to be partial when everyone wants the same thing), and it might seem odd to talk about that as a matter of 'justice' (except insofar as positive-responsiveness is itself seen as one aspect of justice). Those oddities appear only at the limit, however: as we move from limiting cases of 'perfect' to 'partial positive interconnection', genuine issues of impartial justice and real differences among alternative social decision rules reemerge.

One thing that this limiting case serves to emphasize is that positive interconnection among people's votes promotes (perfectly, in the limiting case of perfect positive interconnection) impartiality. Where there is a perfect positive interconnection between people's votes, someone looking at the situation from behind a veil of ignorance-cum-uncertainty would be facing no risk whatsoever: it literally does not matter who he turns out to be; he will end up on the winning side regardless, in a world where everyone votes the same way as everyone else. And as we move from the world of perfect to only partial positive interconnection among people's votes, it remains true that the stronger the positive interconnections the more strongly impartiality is promoted, compared to the baseline case of completely independent voters.

Partial Positive Interconnection

An informal statement

Complete conformism is of course a limiting case. It is possible for people to be more or less likely to mimic one another's votes or thoughts, without that likelihood being an absolute certainty. Those cases are explored more formally below. But casual inspection suggests that democratic truth-tracking and democratic justice-tracking behave somewhat differently in these intermediate cases.

If people's votes are partly but not completely interconnected, democracy will still reliably track the truth, just so long as the size of the electorate is sufficiently large. The stronger the interconnection, the larger the electorate needs to be to achieve any given odds of the collective verdict being correct. But in large electorates, there can be reasonably large interconnections among votes without compromising the truth-tracking power of democracy very much.

The tendency of democracy to maximize impartial want-satisfaction, in contrast, seems much more sensitive to the strength of the interconnections among people's votes and much less sensitive to the size of the electorate.

More formally

To explore the case of a partial but not perfect positive connection between my vote and everyone else's votes, let us introduce the conditional probability $p_{øv_i|øv_1}$ that voter v_i ($i \neq 1$) will vote for ø, given that some reference voter v_1 votes for ø. (In the case where every voter has to vote for one of the two options, it is necessarily the case that $p_{øv_i|øv_1} = 1 - p_{\text{not-}øv_i|øv_1}$.) For convenience, I assume this is the same as the conditional probability that others will vote for not-ø, given that voter v_1 votes for not-ø (that is, $p_{\text{not-}øv_i|\text{not-}øv_1} = p_{øv_i|øv_1}$). Initially, I shall also assume that $p_{øv_i|øv_1}$ is the same for every voter v_i in the society, although I shall go on to relax that assumption below.

The values of $p_{øv_i|øv_1}$ fall between $0 \geq p_{øv_i|øv_1} \geq 1$. The upper bound of that range, $p_{øv_i|øv_1} = 1$, represents the case of complete conformism: the case of perfect positive connection discussed in Section 3.1 above. The bottom of that range represents the case in which all other voters v_i vote opposite to the way voter v_1 votes, because v_1 votes that way. In this section, I am considering the case of partial positive interconnections, so I shall confine my attention in this section to cases where $p_{øv_i|øv_1} > p_{\text{not-}øv_i|øv_1}$.

In the case of statistically independent voters, as envisaged by the 'standard' case for the Condorcet Jury and Majority Rule Theorems, there is no deliberate connection between one person's vote and another's. I am no more, and no less, likely to vote for ø given that you vote ø than I would have been had you voted not-ø. The conditional probability of statistically independent voters v_i voting for ø, given that voter v_1 voted ø, is therefore just the same as their probability of voting ø regardless of what voter v_1 does. In this case of statistically independent voters, then, $p_{\emptyset v_i|\emptyset v_1} = p$.

Now, if v_1 votes for ø, then the probability that each other voter v_i will also vote for ø is $p_{\emptyset v_i|\emptyset v_1}$ and the probability that each other voter will vote for not-ø is, in the two-option case, $(1 - p_{\emptyset v_i|\emptyset v_1})$. By the same token, if v_1 votes for not-ø, then the probability that each other voter v_i will also vote for not-ø is likewise $p_{\emptyset v_i|\emptyset v_1}$ and the probability that each other voter will vote for ø is $(1 - p_{\emptyset v_i|\emptyset v_1})$.

Suppose v_1 votes for ø. Then only $w - 1$ additional votes out of the $N - 1$ remaining votes will be required for ø to win. If v_i votes ø then everyone else's probability of voting ø is $p_{\emptyset v_i|\emptyset v_1}$ and the probability of ø winning ($P\emptyset$) then becomes:

$$P_\emptyset = \sum_{i=w-1}^{N-1} [(N-1)!/(N-1-i)!i!]\, (p_{\emptyset v_i|\emptyset v_1})^i\, (1 - p_{\emptyset v_i|\emptyset v_1})^{N-1-i}$$

(6.3)

As in equation (6.2), voter v_1's probability of winning (Pw) is a function of (a) the probability of voter v_1 supporting ø and the majority of voters also supporting ø and (b) of the probability of voter v_1 supporting not-ø and the majority of voters also supporting not-ø. So next suppose voter v_1 votes for not-ø. Again, only $w - 1$ additional votes out of the $N - 1$ remaining votes would then be required for voter v_1's preferred outcome (here, not-ø) to win. If voter v_1 votes not-ø then everyone else's probability of voting not-ø is once again $p_{\emptyset v_i|\emptyset v_1}$. That makes the probability of not-ø winning $P_{\text{not-}\emptyset}$ given that voter v_1 votes not-ø the same as $P_\emptyset$ as described in equation (6.3). Substituting those values into equation (6.2) makes Pw equal $P\emptyset$ as described in equation (6.3), for the 'partial positive connection' case here under discussion.

The nearer $p_{\emptyset v_i|\emptyset v_1}$ is to one, the nearer the situation will be to that of the limiting case of perfect positive interconnection described above. That has clear consequences for the truth-tracking power of majority rule. Assuming voter competence (in the model sketched here, the competence of the crucial voter v_1 whose lead others follow) $p > 0.5$, the probability of simple majority outcomes being correct lies between p and one. It is nearer to p where $p_{\emptyset v_i|\emptyset v_1}$ is nearer one or N is low. It is nearer to one where $p_{\emptyset v_i|\emptyset v_1}$ is nearer p (that is, nearer the situation is to one of statistically independent voters) and N is high.

Next consider the consequences of partial positive interconnections for the Majority Rule Theorem. In the limiting case of $p_{\emptyset v_i|\emptyset v_1} = 1$ the probability of winning $P_w = 1$. (That is the case of perfect positive interconnection described above.) For values of $p_{\text{øvi|øv1}} < 1$, everything depends on where $p_{\text{øvi|øv1}}$ lies in relation to the majority requirement m. By parity of reasoning to that above, as N approaches infinity P_w approaches one if $p_{\text{øvi|øv1}} > m$ and zero if $p_{\text{øvi|øv1}} < m$.

If they are sufficiently strong, partial positive interconnection can turn losers into winners. By definition, in cases of partial positive interconnection, $p_{\text{øvi|øv1}} > p$. The partial positive interconnection among votes makes the crucial difference between winning and losing only in the interval $p_{\text{øvi|øv1}} > m > p$. It makes no difference, however, in cases where $p > m$ or $p_{\text{øvi|øv1}} < m$: voter v_1 would have been virtually certain to have been on the winning side anyway in the first case, and in the second he is virtually certain to lose anyway (at least in the limiting case as N approaches infinity). Sample calculations, again, suggest that only moderately large electorates – numbering in the thousands, say – are required to make those outcomes virtually certain, even for values of $p_{\text{øvi|øv1}}$ and p only slightly to those sides of m.

Note also that for this case of partial but uniform intercorrelation among everyone's votes, the arguments offered above for the superiority of simple majority rule ($m = 0.5$) still remain valid.

DIVERSITY: SOCIAL CLUSTERS

The above remarks describe what happens where there are *uniform* interconnections among people's votes. Finally, let us consider what happens where there is clustering: where there are distinct groups of people, internally unified (with strong positive interconnections among the votes of group members) but externally diverse (with no or low or maybe even negative interconnections with the votes of members of other groups). At its extreme, this 'unity and diversity' scenario depicts a classically 'segmented society', starkly divided into two or more opposing camps: white versus black, capital versus labour, Catholics versus Protestants, or whatever.

These cases are discussed more formally below. But, informally, it is clear that where society is strongly segmented in such ways both arguments for democracy may well collapse.

If the clusters are tightly unified (to the point of absolute conformity within), then the effective number of distinct points of view for purposes of Condorcet Jury Theorem calculations drops to just the number of different clusters. If that number is small (in the limiting case, if society is polarized into just two opposing groups), the truth-tracking power of democracy practiced across that society is not appreciably greater than the odds of any given individual in each of the groups being right on his or her own.

Similarly, if the clusters are unified to the point of internal absolute conformity, then democracy – far from maximizing the chances of winning impartially for everyone – makes people in some clusters persistent winners and those in others persistent losers.

Formalizing Clustered Interrelationships

The formalisms employed so far assume that whatever connections there might be among people's votes, the connection is the same across the entire electorate. A more complex set of cases concern clustered interconnections of votes. In these cases, there are interconnections among the votes of people *within* the same group which are different from the interconnections (if any) among members of *different* groups. For convenience, I shall continue to assume that the internal connections within groups are always positive (so once again I assume $p_{\varnothing v_i|\varnothing v1} > p_{\text{not-}\varnothing v_i|\varnothing v1}$), and I shall examine what happens when connections across different groups are either positive or negative or non-existent.

Here as before, the 'internal' interconnection between the votes of persons within the same group g_i represents the conditional probability that each other voter v_i in that group will vote ø, given that the reference voter (voter v_1 in group g_1, and so on) votes ø. For convenience, I shall continue to assume that this is the same as the conditional probability that each other voter v_i in that group will vote not-ø, given that voter v_1 votes not-ø (that is, $p_{\text{not-}\varnothing v_i|\text{not-}\varnothing v1} = p_{\varnothing v_i|\varnothing v1}$). For convenience of modelling, I shall further assume that this value is the same within all groups g_i.

The 'external' interconnection represents the conditional probability that people will intentionally mimic the votes of people in groups not their own. In the case of a 'positive external interconnection' the conditional probability that members of groups not my own will vote for ø, given that I vote for ø (and for not-ø, given that I vote for not-ø) is greater than the probability they will vote not-ø, given that I vote for ø (and for ø, given that I vote for not-ø). In the case of 'negative external interconnection' that inequality is reversed.

Here I shall examine the situation from the point of view of group g_1 of which voter v_1 is a member. I shall be asking what is the conditional probability $p_{\varnothing g_i|\varnothing v1}$ that people in other groups g_i ($i \neq 1$) will vote ø, given that voter v_1 votes ø. Again, for convenience I assume $p_{\varnothing g_i|\varnothing v1} = p_{\text{not-}\varnothing g_i|\text{not-}\varnothing v1}$. Again for convenience, I assume that $p_{\varnothing g_i|\varnothing v1}$ is the same for all groups g_i ($i \neq 1$).[23]

The case of 'uniform partial positive interconnection' above corresponds to the case where $p_{\varnothing g_i|\varnothing v1} = p_{\varnothing v_i|\varnothing v1} > p_{\text{not-}\varnothing g_i|\varnothing v1}$. (That is to say, there is exactly the same intentional interconnection of votes between groups as within groups, and those interconnections are of a positive sort.) The cases I next consider hold $p_{øvi|øv1}$ constant but allow $p_{øgi|øv1}$ to vary.

Independent Groups

Take first the simplest case. Imagine there are G groups $\{g_1, g_2, \ldots, g_G\}$. Suppose there is complete conformity ($p_{øvi|øv1} = 1$) *within* each of those groups, but that there is no intentional interconnection in either direction *between* groups (so $p_{øgi|øv1} = p$). Call that the case of 'independent groups'.

The implications of clustering of that sort for the Condorcet Jury Theorem depend, once again, on the magnitudes of N and p, in the ways described above. The only difference is that the number the Condorcet Jury Theorem calculations operates upon is the number G of independent groups rather than the number N of voters (who are here *ex hypothesi* non-independent and purely conformist, within each group). If there are enough groups which are independent of one another in this way, that can do something to compensate for interconnections of opinion within the groups.

The standard Condorcet Jury Theorem as described above corresponds to one limiting case, that of statistically independent voters where $p_{øvi|øv1} = p_{øgi|øv1} = p$. Another limiting case is one of perfect positive connection $p_{øvi|øv1} = 1$ among all members within each of G equal-sized groups, but no intentional connection between the groups (so $p_{øgi|øv1} = p$). In that latter case, the probability of a simple majority verdict tracking the truth is just the probability associated with a majority among an electorate of size G doing so. That is to say, in equation (6.1) N is in this case replaced with G.

It remains formally true, here as before, that as G approaches infinity, the probability that a majority of G will support true propositions approaches certainty, as long as the probability of each group independently supporting true propositions exceeds $p > 0.5$. In practice, however, the number of distinct groups of the sort here in view is unlikely to be very high. And where values of G are small (two to five, say), the probability that a majority vote among them will track the truth is only somewhat higher than the probability of each of them independently tracking the truth on its own.

The Majority Rule Theorem can be recast analogously for cases of clustering of this sort. In the limiting case just described (that is, $p_{øvi|øv1} = 1$ and $p_{øgi|øv1} = p$), we can model each independent group as a single voter, as N approaches infinity. Once again, the probability of any group (and hence the voters associated with it) being on the winning side is maximized and the risk minimized by simple majority rule, $m = 0.5$.

Positively Interconnected Groups

The case of a partial positive interconnections among groups ($p_{øgi|øv1} >$ $p_{not\text{-}øgi|øv1}$) is just a variation on the case discussed above. Conclusions parallel the ones reported there.

Negatively Interconnected Groups

More interesting is the case of negatively intentionally interconnected groups. This would be a classically 'divided society': not only are people partitioned into different groups; those groups also have distinctive patterns of preferences which are, to some greater or lesser extent, *opposed* to one another. People in one group will be more inclined to vote against proposition ø, precisely because people in some other group voted for it.

For ease of analysis, suppose that each group is internally perfectly cohesive, with $p_{øvi|øv1} = 1$. But suppose that the other groups are at least partially intentionally opposed to our reference voter v_1 and hence his group g_1. If our reference voter v_1 votes ø, that does more to make people in opposing groups oppose ø than to support it ($p_{not\text{-}øgi|øv1} > p_{øgi|øv1}$). In that case, we also know that $p_{not\text{-}øgi|øv1} > 1-p$, the latter being the probability that people would vote not-ø were their votes statistically independent of one another. Let us see what then happens as $p_{not\text{-}øgi|øv1}$ increases toward its limit of one.[24]

Consider first the implications of a divided society for the truth-tracking power of simple majority rule. The first thing to say, of course, is this: assuming N (the number of individuals) is much larger than G (the number of groups), the probability of the majority verdict being correct is much more strongly affected by p and $p_{øvi|øv1}$ than it is by $p_{not\text{-}øgi|øv1}$.

In the limiting case under discussion, $p_{øvi|øv1} = 1$ there are in effect only G independent points of view, for purposes of Condorcet Jury Theorem calculations. As commented above, that reduces the truth-tracking power of majority rule considerably, in itself. But add to that the further fact that $p_{not\text{-}øgi|øv1} > p$, and that makes matters worse yet again. Now, we do not even have G fully independent points of view represented: rather, the number of independent voters is reduced to a fraction of that, to $p_{not\text{-}øgi|øv1} G$ to be precise.

The Condorcet Jury Theorem in its classic form described above presupposes that votes are statistically independent of one another. Deviation from independence in either direction – positive ($p_{øgi|øv1} > p$) or, as here, negative ($p_{not\text{-}øgi|øv1} > 1-p$) – undermines the truth-tracking power of majority rule in just the same fashion. Interconnections between voters, whether positive or negative, effectively reduce the number of independent perspectives, and that is what is crucial to the Condorcet Jury Theorem.

Consider next the implications of negatively intentionally interconnected groups for majority rule's capacity to promote justice, understood as impartial want-satisfaction. Informally, it is easy enough to see what is going to happen. In the limiting case in which people in all other groups are certain to vote the opposite way to voter v_1 (that is, $p_{\text{not-øgı|øvı}} = 1$), voter v_1 (and hence his group g_1) will be on the winning side only if he succeeds in collecting enough votes from within his own group to win (that is, $g_1 p_{øvı|øvı} > m$). Since $0 \leq p_{øvı|øvı} \leq 1$, that inequality can only ever be satisfied if group g_1 is a 'majority faction' (that is, $g_1 > m$); and even then, it is likely to be satisfied only for ones that are internally pretty cohesive (that is, high $p_{øvı|øvı}$). 'Minority factions' (that is, $g_1 < m$), even where internally cohesive, can virtually never hope to win when other groups take a strongly negative intentional orientation toward them in their voting.[25]

Were voters uncertain which group they would be in, the risk of finding themselves among such an almost-certainly-losing 'minority faction' would be something they would want to minimize. Real-world voters of course often know exactly what side they are on in an actual divided society, and opt for one decision rule rather than some other on the basis of that knowledge. But that is a reflection of partiality: precisely the sort of thing that maximizing justice understood as 'impartial want-satisfaction' is supposed to rule out.

Finally, note that simple majority rule would still be the best decision rule, even from the point of view of the smaller group in such a society. That is obviously so, assuming decision rules of a symmetrical form: there, requiring a special majority $m > 0.5$ would make it even *harder* for the smaller group to achieve the requisite majority, after all (McGann, 2004). But even 'asymmetrical special majority rules' only improve the chances of the smaller group getting the outcome it wants if that group's preferred outcome gets identified as the 'default option'. From the point of view of the uncertain voter (who is here being used as the touchstone of maximum impartial want-satisfaction) the 'default option' is as likely as not to be something other than what that voter prefers.

Thus, democracy (understood as simple majority rule) is still arguably the best decision rule even for a deeply divided society. It is merely the case that, under those conditions, democracy does not deliver nearly as much justice (that is, impartial want-satisfaction) as it does under conditions of societies of purely independent individuals ($p_{øvı|øvı} = p$) or independent groups ($p_{øgı|øvı} = p$) or positively cohesive societies ($p_{øvı|øvı} > p$ or $p_{øgı|øvı} > p$).

Probability of Winning: a More Formal Statement

One way to pull together the strands of this argument relating to the probability of uncertain voters winning under varying circumstances is to observe that, at the limit as N and g_1 approach infinity, voter v_1 will be on the winning side of the election if and only if

$$g_1 p_{øvi|øv1} + (N - g_1) p_{øgi|øv1} > w \tag{6.4}$$

where g_1 is the number of voters in group g_1, N is the total number of voters, w is the absolute number of voters required to win, $p_{øvi|øv1}$ is the conditional probability that other members of g_1 vote ø given that voter v_1 votes ø, and $p_{øgi|øv1}$ is the conditional probability that members of other groups g_i ($i \neq 1$) vote ø given that voter v_1 in group g_1 votes ø.

The case of completely independent voters, envisaged in the standard versions of the Condorcet Jury Theorem and the Majority Rule Theorem, corresponds to the case in which $p_{øvi|øv1} = p_{øgi|øv1} = p$. Substituting p into equation (6.4) for those other values yields the conclusion that voter v_1 will be on the winning side if and only if $pN > w$ – which is to say (recalling $m = w/N$) if and only if $p > m$. That is as reported above.

The above case of partially positively interconnected individuals not organized into groups corresponds to the case in which $p_{øvi|øv1} > p$. There is only one group, so $g_1 = N$ and $p_{øgi|øv1}$ is in this case undefined (and in any case irrelevant, since it gets multiplied by zero in equation (6.4). Substituting into equation (6.4) and rearranging terms, that yields the conclusion that voter v_1 will be on the winning side if and only if $p_{øvi|øv1} N > w$. Comparing this to the condition required for voter v_1 to win in the baseline case of completely independent voters, $pN > w$, the left side of the above equation is always greater than for the baseline equation (since in the case here in view, $p_{øvi|øv1} > p$). Hence it is unambiguously easier for voter v_1 to win in the case of positively interconnected but ungrouped voters than it is in the case of completely independent voters.

Let us turn now to cases of clustering. The first example is that of independent groups, completely unified within but completely independent of one another. That is to say, $p_{øgi|øv1} = p$; and in the case considered above, we assumed for convenience $p_{øvi|øv1} = 1$. Substituting into equation (6.4) and rearranging terms, that yields the conclusion that voter v_1 will be on the winning side if and only if $pN > w - g_1(1 - p)$. In effect, the number of votes it takes for voter v_1 to win is thus reduced, compared to the baseline scenario of completely independent voters; by how much depends on how far p is below one and on the size of his group g_1.

The second and third types of clustering involve positively interconnected groups and negatively interconnected groups, respectively. For convenience, we assumed in both of the above cases that $p_{øvi|øv1} = 1$. Substituting that into equation (6. 4) and rearranging terms yields the conclusion that voter v_1 will be on the winning side if and only if

$$p_{ogi\|ov1}N > w - g_1(1 - p_{ogi\|ov1}) \tag{6.5}$$

The condition for voter v_1 winning in the baseline case of completely independent voters, recall, is $pN > w$.

By definition, in positively interconnected groups $p_{ogi\|ov1} > p$. Hence in the case of positively interconnected groups, the left-hand side of equation (6.5) is greater than the left-hand side of the equation for the baseline case; and the right-hand side of equation (6.5) is lower. Hence it is unambiguously easier for voter v_1 to win in the case of positively interconnected groups than in the case of completely independent voters.

In negatively interconnected groups, by definition $p_{ogi\|ov1} < p$. Hence in negatively interconnected groups, the left-hand side of equation (6.5) is less than the left-hand side of the equation for the baseline case; and the right-hand side of equation (6.5) is higher. Hence it is unambiguously more difficult for voter v_1 to win in the case of negatively interconnected groups than in the case of completely independent voters.

Using equation (6.4), we can also perform some sample calculations to get a sense of the way in which in-group unity and cross-group diversity might interact to increase voter v_1's chances of being on the winning side. Equation (6.4) can be rewritten in proportional terms as $(g_1/N)(p_{ovi\|ov1}) + (1 - [g_1/N])(p_{ogi\|ov1}) > m$. Suppose, for example, group g_1 constitutes a quarter of an electorate whose decisions are by simple majority rule. Then voter v_1 will be on the winning side whenever $0.25(p_{ovi\|ov1}) + 0.75(p_{ogi\|ov1}) > 0.5$, implying that to win voter v_1 needs for $p_{ogi\|ov1}$ to be at least 0.333 (even when his group is completely behind him, $p_{ovi\|ov1} = 1$) and maybe as high as 0.66 (when his own group is totally opposed to him, $p_{ovi\|ov1} = 0$). If g_1 constitutes a tenth of total electorate, to win voter v_1 needs for $p_{ogi\|ov1}$ to be at least 0.44 (when $p_{ovi\|ov1} = 1$), rising to 0.56 (when $p_{ovi\|ov1} = 0$).

Impartiality with Clusters

In our standard of 'justice' as 'maximizing impartial want satisfaction', the discussion so far concentrates on the 'maximizing want satisfaction' aspect of that desideratum.

Issues of 'impartiality' can be explored here, as previously, through the lens of voter behind a veil of ignorance-cum-uncertainty: here, uncertainty over which group he would turn out to be in. As suggested above, the magnitude of the risk he faces, depending on which group he turns out to be in, can be measured as the difference in the probability of his getting what he wants if he turns out to be in one group rather than another. And here as before, what appears intrapersonally as 'risk' appears interpersonally as a deviation from 'impartiality'.

In the case of negatively interconnected groups discussed above, for example, the risk is at a maximum. Where all groups are completely unified internally, if the voter turns out to be a member of a group larger than the required majority m he will win with probability one; and if he turns out to be a member of a group smaller than m, he has zero chance of winning.

In the case of positively interconnected groups discussed above, in contrast, the risk is lessened. Here again, it is assumed that all groups are again completely unified internally. But here, they act partially in sympathy with one another. Even if the voter there turns out to be a member of a relatively small group, the propensity of other groups to vote in sympathy with his group will increase the chances he will end up winning, compared to the baseline case of completely independent, ungrouped voters. Where all groups vote in sympathy with all others in this way, it makes less difference to a person's prospects of winning which group he turns out to be in.

The case of independent groups discussed above falls somewhere in between those other two cases. There, it is assumed that there is some interconnection among voters within the group, but that there is no interconnection whatsoever among groups. A voter's chances of winning are increased by the positive interconnections with other voters in the same group, of course; so his chances of winning in the case of independent groups is increased, relative to the baseline case of completely independent, ungrouped voters. (That is equally true of the interconnections among voters within groups in the previous two cases, of course.) But in the case of independent groups, there is nothing to exacerbate (as with negatively interconnected groups) or to alleviate (as with positively interconnected ones) the effects of turning out to be in one group rather than another. The risk faced by the uncertain voter in the case of independent groups thus falls in between the risks he faces in those other two cases.

CONCLUSION

In short:

- In individualistic societies, where each person decides how to vote completely independently of any one else, democracy (specifically, simple majority rule) can indeed be counted on to promote both truth and justice, understood as impartial want-satisfaction.
- In conformist societies, democracy is more just but also less truth-apt.
- In divided societies composed of opposing groups, democracy cannot be relied upon to track either truth or justice.

In assessing which social decision rule is best, Churchill's telling quip remains apposite. There is no reason in the arguments given here for thinking that any other system of government could do any better than democracy (simple majority rule) in promoting either truth or justice, even in a divided society.

The point remains that, in a divided society, even that best social decision rule delivers both less truth and less justice than it does in more individualist sorts of societies where people vote more independently of one another. The same apparatus that formally establishes the superiority of simple majority rule in promoting truth and justice also establishes the inferiority of divided societies in respect of the truth or justice that is socially achievable through that best decision rule.

NOTES

* Ideas feeding into this chapter were presented to a conference at the Kyoto Institute for the Integrated Study of Future Generations as well as at the conference in honour of Geoff Brennan at the Ministry of the Economy and Finance, Rome. I am grateful for comments, then and later, from Richard Bradley, Geoff Brennan, John Dunn, Dave Estlund, Jim Flynn, Raymond Geuss, Hartmut Kliemt, Pratap Metha, Philip Pettit and, most particularly, Christian List.

† Professor of philosophy and social & political theory, Research School of Social Sciences, Australian National University, Canberra ACT 0200, Australia <goodinb@coombs. anu.edu.au>.

1. Brennan and Buchanan (1980, 1985), Brennan and Hamlin (2000), Brennan and Lomasky (1989, 1993), Brennan and Pettit (1990, 2004).

2. In the formal sections of this chapter I confine my attention to the simplest sorts of cases, involving choice between just two options. What I here say about simple majority rule in the two-option can often also be proven to be true of plurality rule in the case of more than two options (List and Goodin, 2001; Goodin and List, 2006).

3. It does not even really satisfy one's preferences over truths. Treating something you wish to be true *as if* it were true does not, in itself, *make* it true.

4. Mill (1859), ch. 2.

5. Milton (1644/1963), p. 58.

6. Holmes (1919), Coase (1974).

7. The arguments of these two paragraphs are elaborated at greater length in Sparrow and Goodin (2001).

8. 'Intellectual property' adheres not to ideas as such but embodiments of them, in a text or description of a manufacturing process filed with the copyright office.

9. Aristotle (1946), bk. 3, ch. 11, Waldron (1999), ch. 5.

10. Condorcet (1785/1972), pp. 279 ff. This result is arguably what Rousseau had in mind in bk. 2, ch. 3 of *Social Contract*, but if so that presents the proof in badly garbled form. On the relation between Condorcet and Roussseau, see Grofman and Feld (1988); compare Estlund et al. (1989).

11. Barry (1964), p. 9. See also Barry (1965), pp. 292–3; Black (1958), pp. 163–5.

12. And errors (votes for 'wrong' options) are randomly distributed; or in any case, each voter is more likely to vote for the correct proposition than for any other.

13. The first result is from Grofman, Owen and Feld (1983); the rest are from List and Goodin (2001).

14. Black (1958), p. 163. See further Goodin (2003), ch. 7.
15. In the two-option case – more likely to be right than random ($1/k$) in the k-option case.
16. Instead of assuming that the value of p (and various conditional probabilities introduced in Sections 3 and 4 below) are identical for everyone, we can equivalently assume that those values represent the means of a symmetrical distribution across the population. The same results will then still obtain just so long as the distribution is symmetrical around the mean.
17. See Dowding, Goodin and Pateman (2004) for a sample of ways in which the connections might be drawn.
18. Compare, for example, Rawls (1967) and Beitz (1989).
19. Here again, m is the actual number of votes required to decide an issue, in either of the ways described below; but once again, m is an increasing function of N (the precise details of which vary depending of the variety of 'special majority rule' adopted).
20. As specified by, for example, May (1952), who famously proved that simple majority rule was the unique decision rule that was both 'positively responsive' (that is, want-satisfying) and 'impartial' in those two respects over a universal domain.
21. Submajority rules ($m < 0.5$) can be used in a variety ways, primarily to force an assembly to bring an issue to a vote (Vermuele, 2005). But they cannot be coherently, non-arbitrarily used to determine the final resolution of an issue.
22. This further stipulation is important. After all, if p is high then there is a high likelihood that everyone will vote the same way as everyone else – not because they are mimicking one another intentionally, but merely because they are independently tracking the same thing ('truth', 'desirable outcomes', and so on). That sort of intercorrelation of votes does not violate the 'independence' assumption built into the Condorcet Jury or Majority Rule Theorems, of course. It is only the deliberate 'tracking' of one another's votes – making your vote conditional on theirs – that violates the independence assumption in those models. See Estlund (1994) and, on 'tracking' more generally, Nozick (1981).
23. Rewriting $p_{øgỉ|øvl}$ to index the conditional probability to the relevant reference person in each group, as voter v_1 is for group g_1 in this expression.
24. Empirically, Brubaker (2002, p. 164) rightly complains of the fallacy he calls 'groupism': 'the tendency to take discrete, sharply differentiated, internally homogenous and externally bounded groups as basic constituents of social life, chief protagonists of social conflicts and fundamental units of social analysis'. I appreciate the irony of building precisely those assumptions into a rational-choice model whose 'methodological and ontological individualism' ought in principle inoculate it against those errors (Brubaker, 2002, p. 165). Still, modelling inevitably rests on simplifying assumptions. Elsewhere I have attempted to sketch some rational-choice foundations for such as these (Goodin, 2003, ch. 2), and I hope to be able to elaborate those models more fully in the future.
25. These mathematics confirm whatever organizer knows: a minority faction is only likely to beat a larger group intentionally opposed to it if the minority faction is more internally cohesive than is its larger opponent.

REFERENCES

Aristotle (1946), *Politics*, trans. and ed. Ernest Barker, Oxford: Clarendon Press.
Barry, Brian (1964), 'The public interest', *Proceedings of the Aristotelian Society (Supplement)*, **38**, 1–18.
Barry, Brian (1965), *Political Argument*, London: Routledge & Kegan Paul.
Beitz, Charles R. (1989), *Political Equality*, Princeton, NJ: Princeton University Press.
Black, Duncan (1958), *The Theory of Committees and Elections*, Cambridge: Cambridge University Press.

Brennan, Geoffrey and James M. Buchanan (1980), *The Power to Tax: Analytical Foundations of a Fiscal Constitution*, Cambridge: Cambridge University Press.

Brennan, Geoffrey and James M. Buchanan (1985), *The Reason of Rules: Constitutional Political Economy*, Cambridge: Cambridge University Press.

Brennan, Geoffrey and Alan Hamlin (2000), *Democratic Devices and Desires*, Cambridge: Cambridge University Press.

Brennan, Geoffrey and Loren Lomasky (eds) (1989), *Politics and Process: New Essays in Democratic Thought*, Cambridge: Cambridge University Press.

Brennan, Geoffrey and Loren Lomasky (1993), *Democracy and Decision: The Pure Theory of Electoral Preference*, Cambridge: Cambridge University Press.

Brennan, Geoffrey and Philip Pettit (1990), 'Unveiling the vote', *British Journal of Political Science*, **20**, 311–34.

Brennan, Geoffrey and Philip Pettit (2004), *The Economy of Esteem: An Essay on Civil and Political Society*, Oxford: Oxford University Press.

Brubaker, Rogers (2002), 'Ethnicity without groups', *Archives Europeénnes de Sociologie*, **43**, 163–89.

Buchanan, James M. and Gordon Tullock (1962), *The Calculus of Consent*, Ann Arbor: University of Michigan Press.

Coase, R.H. (1974), 'The market for goods and the market for ideas', *American Economic Review (Papers & Proceedings)*, **64** (2), 384–402.

Condorcet, Marquis de (1785), *Essai sur l'application de l'analyse à la probabilité des décisions rendues à la pluralité des voix*, Paris: l'Imprimerie Royale; fascimile edition New York: Chelsea, 1972.

Dowding, Keith, Robert E. Goodin and Carole Pateman (eds) (2004), *Justice and Democracy: Essays for Brian Barry*, Cambridge: Cambridge University Press.

Edgeworth, Francis Y. (1925), 'The pure theory of taxation', in *Papers Relating to Political Economy*, London: Macmillan, vol. 2, pp. 100–116.

Elster, Jon (1983), *Sour Grapes*, Cambridge: Cambridge University Press.

Estlund, David (1994), 'Opinion leaders, independence and Condorcet's jury theorem', *Theory and Decision*, **36**, 131–62.

Estlund, David, Jeremy Waldron, Bernard Grofman and Scott Feld (1989), 'Democratic theory and the public interest: Condorcet and Rousseau revisited', *American Political Science Review*, **83**, 1317–40.

Goodin, Robert E. (1976), *The Politics of Rational Man*, London: Wiley.

Goodin, Robert E. (2003), *Reflective Democracy*, Oxford: Oxford University Press.

Goodin, Robert E. and Christian List (2005), 'Special majorities rationalized', *British Journal of Political Science*, forthcoming.

Goodin, Robert E. and Christian List (2006), 'In partial praise of the plurality rule: generalizing May's theorem in an informationally impoverished environment', mimeo, Social and Political Theory Program, Research School of Social Sciences, Australian National University.

Grofman, Bernard and Scott L. Feld (1988), 'Rosseau's general will: a Condorcetian perspective', *American Political Science Review*, **82**, 567–76.

Grofman, Bernard, Guillermo Owen and Scott L. Feld (1983), 'Thirteen theorems in search of the truth', *Theory and Decision*, **15**, 261–78.

Harsanyi, John C. (1953), 'Cardinal utility in welfare economics and in the theory of risk-taking', *Journal of Political Economy*, **61**, 434–5.

Harsanyi, John C. (1982), 'Morality and the theory of rational behaviour', in Amartya Sen and Bernard Williams (eds), *Utilitarianism and Beyond*, Cambridge: Cambridge University Press, pp. 39–62.

Hicks, John R. (1941), 'The rehabilitation of consumers' surplus', *Review of Economics Studies*, **8**, 108–16.

Holmes, Oliver Wendell Jr. (1919), 'Dissenting opinion', *Abrams v. United States*, 250 US 616.

List, Christian and Robert E. Goodin (2001), 'Epistemic democracy: generalizing the Condorcet jury theorem', *Journal of Political Philosophy*, **9**, 277–306.

May, Kenneth O. (1952), 'A set of independent, necessary and sufficient conditions for simple majority decision', *Econometrica*, **20**, 680–84.

McGann, A.J. (2004), 'The tyranny of the supermajority: how majority rule protects minorities', *Journal of Theoretical Politics*, **16**, 53–78.

Mill, James (1823), 'Essay on government', reprinted in Terence Ball (ed.) (1992), *James Mill: Political Writings*, Cambridge: Cambridge University Press.

Mill, John Stuart (1859), *On Liberty*, Harmondsworth, Mddx: Pengiun, 1974.

Milton, John (1644), *Areopagitica*, London: Macmillan, 1963.

Nozick, Robert (1981), *Philosophical Explanations*, Cambridge, Mass: Harvard University Press.

Rae, Douglas W. (1969), 'Decision-rules and individual values in constitutional choice', *American Political Science Review*, **63**, 40–56.

Rae, Douglas W. (1975), 'The limits of consensual decision', *American Political Science Review*, **69**, 1270–94.

Rawls, John (1967), 'Legal obligation and the duty of fair play', in Sidney Hook (ed.), *Law and Philosophy*, New York: New York University Press, pp. 3–18.

Rawls, John (1971), *A Theory of Justice*, Cambridge, Mass: Harvard University Press.

Rousseau, Jean-Jacques (1763), *Social Contract*, reprinted in G.D.H. Cole (trans. & ed.) (1973), *The Social Contract and Discourses*, London: Everyman/Dent, pp. 164–278.

Sparrow, Robert and Robert E. Goodin (2001), 'The competition of ideas: market or garden?' *CRISPP (Critical Review of International Social and Political Philosophy)*, **4**, 45–58.

Straffin, Philip D. Jr. (1977), 'Majority rule and general decision rules', *Theory and Decision*, **8**, 351–60.

Taylor, Michael (1969), 'Proof of a theorem majority rule', *Behavioral Science*, **14**, 228–31.

Vermuele, Adrian (2005), 'Submajority rules: forcing accountability upon majorities', *Journal of Political Philosophy*, **13**, 74–98.

Waldron, Jeremy (1999), *The Dignity of Legislation*, Cambridge: Cambridge University Press.

7.   Error-dependent norms
Philip Pettit

Many norms appear to arise, or at least to stabilize and fixate, as a result of an error on people's parts as to the attitudes of others. Geoffrey Brennan and I have talked about this possibility a number of times and touched on it in our recent book (Brennan and Pettit, 2004). The topic is of the kind that appeals to his puzzle-centered, paradox-savoring mind, and I hope that he will appreciate an independent discursus on it as a contribution to this welcome celebration of his work.

My discussion will be in four sections. I look in turn at the definition of norms; at how, under this definition, a norm can be based on an error shared among those who observe it; at the psychological plausibility of such an error; and finally at the sorts of norms that are likely to be supported, for good or ill, in this way. The discussion draws, particularly in the earlier sections, on earlier work, the bulk of it done in collaboration with Geoff (Pettit, 1990; Brennan and Pettit, 1993, 2000, 2004).

THE DEFINITION OF NORMS

The word 'norm', as used in characterization of society, has two more or less obvious connotations. First, anything that deserves to be described as a norm of a society – an actual, not a would-be, norm – has to be a regularity that prevails there: a pattern of behavior that characterizes the society, marking it off from actual or potential competitors. But, second, the regularity in question cannot be a matter of indifference amongst the people who sustain it. In order to have the status of a norm, a social regularity has to be seen, however tacitly, as something with a certain sort of normative claim on people's allegiance: as something that, for whatever reason, is appropriate in relevant contexts; it has to attract approval or the breach of the regularity disapproval.

But these two connotations do not exhaust the associations of the word 'norm', as that is used in social contexts. Suppose that a regularity was behaviorally and attitudinally supported among the members of a certain society but that there was no connection between the attitudinal approval and the behavioral compliance; suppose, in other words, that the attitudinal support was epiphenomenal in relation to the behavioral compliance. In that case the regularity would certainly be something that people had reason to welcome and celebrate, like an aspect of their biology; but it would scarcely count as a regularity that they treated as normative. This suggests that we ought to build a third connotation into our use of the word 'norm'. We ought to stipulate that in order for a regularity to count as a social norm, it should not only be instantiated as a general rule, and not only seen in general as an appropriate regularity to instantiate; in addition, the fact that it is seen as appropriate – the fact that it is approved – should help to explain why it is generally instantiated.

This characterization of social norms is fairly rough, since it leaves open a range of questions. Does a regularity count as generally instantiated if it is a regularity that applies only to those holding a certain office or meeting a certain qualification? How extensive is the pattern of approval envisaged when it is said that the regularity must be seen as appropriate: appropriate morally, or at least prudentially, or at least for someone with this or that goal in mind? Moreover, must the approval be associated with the type of behavior, considered in general, or will it suffice if it just happens instance by instance that the behavior is seen as appropriate? And what, finally, is required for the pattern of approval to help to explain the pattern of behavior? Must it contribute in some measure to the production of the behavior, at least among a number of those complying? Or will it do if it is there to reinforce the behavior, should the motives that normally produce it fail for one or another reason? Will it do, in other words, if it is a virtual or standby force that supports the behavior, rather than an active contributor to people's motivation (Pettit, 1995)?

I am happy to leave aside most of these questions, taking the inclusive view that we should be ready to describe as a social norm any of the large range of regularities in people's behavior that meet some version of our three conditions. Thus a regularity among the members of a society will constitute a norm just in the event that:

- nearly everyone conforms;
- the behavior is nearly always thought appropriate in some way;
- and this attitude helps to explain the general conformity.

I am happy also to leave aside the further question, often raised in this context, as to whether it is essential for a social norm that the fulfillment of the three core conditions is a matter accessible to common knowledge. It will be commonly known that the conditions are fulfilled if each is aware that the conditions are fulfilled; each is aware that each is aware that each

is aware of this; and so on indefinitely, for any question of higher awareness that may arise. I am content that a regularity may count as a social
norm even if it is not accessible to common knowledge in this sense. The
upshot is a generous, perhaps deflationary, sense of social norm. But it is
supported by most recent authors on the subject and ought not to generate
any deep controversy (Hart, 1961; Winch, 1963; Coleman, 1990; Sober and
Wilson, 1998; Elster, 1999).

Norms in this sense often have very welcome effects. They dictate the
ways in which people relate to one another in discourse, generally embracing patterns of honesty, trustworthiness and sincerity; the ways in which
they otherwise seek to influence one another, eschewing resort to violence,
theft, fraud, and coercion; the ways in which they commit themselves con-
scientiously to various collaborative causes, playing the part that is collectively required of them; and the ways in which they conduct their business
and professional lives according to relevant codes of practice.

Such norms are the motors of civil society, leading people to deal well
with one another, even when they are beyond the reach of the law, are
unconstrained by the discipline of self-interest, and are free of the incentives provided by family and related ties. They exemplify the idea of the rule
of obligation introduced by H.L.A. Hart (1961, pp. 84–5) in his classic
study of *The Concept of Law* (see also Ullmann-Margalit, 1977, pp. 12–13).
He characterizes such rules by the fact that they generally prevail in the relevant group, they are supported by serious social pressure, they are thought
useful in some way for the life of the group, and they are individually bur-
densome, however beneficial in group terms.

But norms in the sense defined – the sense that answers to our rough
account – may also be socially neutral or even socially counterproductive,
unlike Hart's rules of obligation. Norms that are socially neutral will include
the sorts of norms that barely enter consciousness, such as those governing
eye-contact and turn-taking in conversation, and the distance at which it is
appropriate to stand in relation to an interlocutor (Goffman, 1975). Socially
counterproductive norms come in a variety of shapes. Some will serve
subcultures well, for example, while serving the society as a whole badly
(McAdams, 1995; Dharmapala and McAdams, 2001). Some will have a
mutually destructive effect as in the norms whereby it becomes obligatory
for people to exact revenge in kind for any harm done to a member of their
family (Elster, 1990; Hardin, 1995; Nisbett and Cohen, 1996). And some will
impose fashions and fads on people who would generally prefer not to be
motivated to embrace them; they represent a tyranny of majoritarian esteem
(McAdams, 1997).

One final comment on this definition of norms, before turning to the
possibility of norms sustained in error. There is no conflict in saying that

a regularity that is a matter of law, being supported by legal penalty, is also a norm; it can satisfy the conditions for being a norm while satisfying also the conditions for being a law. And neither is there any conflict in saying that a regularity that is a matter of convention, say because it solves a coordination predicament to everyone's satisfaction (Lewis, 1969), may also be a norm; again it can consistently satisfy the conditions for belonging in each of those categories. The class of norms to which our definition directs us can overlap, and surely does overlap, with those distinct categories.

THE POSSIBILITY OF ERROR-DEPENDENCE

The definition of norms just given allows for a variety of normative regularities. Norms will vary, for example, depending on factors like the following:

- whether compliance is approved, non-compliance disapproved, or both conditions hold;
- whether the approval involved is a matter of egocentric comfort or advantage or engages a more moralized disposition;
- whether the approved compliance involves successfully achieving something or just trying to do so, as in a norm of aspiration.

I am interested here, however, in a different source of variation in norms. Under the definition offered, it is required that there is a general pattern of approval and that this helps to explain the compliance of each with the regularity in question. But there are a number of ways in which the general pattern of approval may connect with individual compliance and, correspondingly, there are different sorts of norms that the approval may support.

The standard connection, as we might describe it, involves each individual in internalizing the general pattern of approval – coming to share the attitude of approval present in the society at large – and in being led by his or her personal approval into instantiating the regularity. When such an internalized norm is in place, those who conform to it will do so out of personal attachment or conviction to the value in question and will count, by traditional criteria, as agents of virtue.

Some theorists give almost exclusive attention to internalized norms, emphasizing how far internalization supports the stability of normative behavior (Cooter, 1994, 1996). But even if internalization aids stability, it seems scarcely deniable that virtuous, norm-observant behavior may often be supported by something distinct. It may be reinforced – it may be protected from weakness of will and the like – by the fact that if someone does not act in accordance with a received norm, particularly a norm that is socially beneficial, then he or she is going to lose the approval of others, and perhaps attract their disapproval. Assume that for whatever reason, intrinsic or instrumental, people care about enjoying the positive approval of others and avoiding their disapproval (Pettit, 1990; Brennan and Pettit, 2004). In that case it should be clear that if failures of virtue lead to failures of behavior, then people are liable to be punished, however involuntarily, by those others who observe and understand what they have done; they will be punished, at the least, by the withdrawal of approval, or the appearance of disapproval.

There is a long and plausible tradition of thinking that this fact means that in many contexts, virtuous or internalized adherence to norms can be supported and stabilized by collateral incentives. The pursuit of the honorable can be underpinned by the desire to be honored. This tradition may have its origin in the Aristotelian idea that continence – compliance with the right for reasons independent of its rightness – can support and even give rise to virtue proper: to a compliance with right behavior that is a matter of second nature and bespeaks an attachment to the right (Aristotle, 1976). Doing the right thing for the wrong reasons may be a vice: to quote from T.S. Eliot's *Murder in the Cathedral*, it may be 'the greatest treason/To do the right deed for the wrong reason'. But if it is a vice, then it is a saving vice; it represents a form of motivation and behavior that is friendly to virtue, not inimical (Lovejoy, 1961; Brennan and Pettit, 2004).

Once we recognize that people may be motivated by the pursuit of others' approval, rather than by the internalization of that approval, then we are in a position to see that not all norms, however widely instantiated, may be internalized. There are two varieties of non-internalized norms that are possible, in particular.

Given that people are motivated by the desire for the approval of others, the first possibility is that each acts out of that desire, and out of that desire only, without anyone actually having the attitude of approval in question. Everyone, in other words, is mistaken in thinking that others generally approve of a certain form of behavior – they are mistaken about the relevant value adopted by others – yet everyone displays that behavior, believing falsely that this will attract the approval of others. This possibility has been described by psychologists as a case where pluralistic ignorance supports a norm (Miller and Prentice, 1994, 1996).

A good example of a norm supported in pluralistic ignorance – better, perhaps, pluralistic error – is that whereby, according to one study, a group of students tended to comply with a certain regularity in the amount of alcohol consumed on a night out. The study revealed that almost all of the students disapproved of the relatively high level of drinking required under the regularity but abided by that regularity because of mistakenly thinking that others disapproved of lower levels of consumption (see Prentice and Miller, 1993; Schroeder and Prentice, 1998).

Should a regularity supported in such error about the values of others count as a norm, under our definition? It may seem not, since the definition presupposes that the behavior involved attracts approval, or its absence disapproval – that it actually answers to an espoused value – and all that is available in this case is the mistaken expectation of approval or disapproval. But if I believe that everyone else approves of some behavior, even a sort that I myself don't approve of, there is a sense in which I believe that that behavior is appropriate or valuable: it is appropriate according to local standards. So perhaps this regularity should count as a norm under the definition offered. Even if that is not accepted, however, it is surely reasonable to recognize how close to a norm in the strict sense this sort of regularity is and to treat it as a limit case.

So much for the first sort of non-internalized norm. The second variety has not been explicitly recognized in the same way but becomes visible once we recognize that people care about enjoying the approval of others and avoiding their disapproval: for short, care about their approval. It involves error, like the first, but error about a somewhat different issue from that of whether others approve of a certain behavior. In this case, people believe that others approve of the relevant type of behavior, and they are right to do so: they get the values of others right. But here they mistakenly think that it is this personal approval that leads others, in fidelity to their values, to display that behavior. They rightly believe that the others see the behavior as appropriate or valuable, even perhaps required, but they wrongly think that others perform the behavior out of a recognition of its merits in that regard; they mistakenly think that the others are virtuous.

This scenario of error about the virtue of others, as distinct from error about their values, is possible under the hypothesis that people care about the approval of others. For while everyone thinks that others are displaying the normative behavior out of personal virtue – as a result of their personally approving of the behavior – the fact may be that they display that behavior out of a desire to enjoy the approval of others or avoid their disapproval. The scenario is one in which everyone is 'continent' rather than virtuous, doing the right thing for reasons other than that it is right: doing the right thing for the sake of the approval of others. A norm is sustained in people's behavior but it is not internalized by anyone.

The first case of a non-internalized norm not only involved error; it involved error essentially. If students in the drinking example knew that others did not actually hold by the pattern of approval imputed by each, that knowledge might be expected to undermine the norm; and this appears to have been borne out in that actual study. Adherence to the norm in this case is, as we might say, error-dependent: more exactly, it is dependent on the near universality of the error.

Does the second sort of non-internalized norm involve error essentially, in the same way as the first? Is compliance with this norm also likely to be error-dependent? I believe that there is a possible scenario in which it would be.

Imagine that the soldiers in a military unit all display courage in action, that they all approve of courageous behavior and that those two facts are correctly registered in common belief amongst them: each believes that each believes this, and so on. Imagine, next, that they each hold by the equally common belief that the courageous behavior of others testifies to the presence of personal courage – that is, virtue – and that others act as they do out of such courage. But imagine, finally, that this belief is false, since they each act out of the belief that if they act courageously they will be taken to be courageous like the others and that they will attract approval on that account: they will avoid the stigma of being seen as cowards.

In such a situation compliance with the norm is certainly error-dependent: that is, dependent on the near universality of the error. For suppose that this error was not in place, so that it was a matter of common belief that no one is really courageous or virtuous and that they all behave courageously, if they do, out of a wish to be seen as courageous. In that case, not only will there not be a motive of courage to drive the soldiers to behave courageously, neither will the motive of seeking a reputation for courage be present; or neither at least will it be effective. For no one will be able to think that others will take them to be courageous just because they behave courageously. Behaving courageously will not be supported, then, in the motivations of the parties and, short of an awareness of this absence of motive generating some further transformation – which it well may do – courageous behavior will vanish. We can imagine an information cascade in which the awareness that there is no reputational gain in acting courageously – in particular, no shame in failing to do so – rapidly spreads to the point where almost no one remains disposed to act that way; there is mutiny in the ranks.

One final comment. In both the cases we have considered the error made is made by everyone. That is a particularly dramatic and clear-cut sort of situation but it is worth mentioning that error-dependence may also come in degrees. A norm may come to be maintained, not in virtue of universal error on some matter, but in virtue of a certain level of error, whether about attitudes or dispositions. In this chapter I abstract from a consideration of such cases, however, as they would take me too far afield. I focus on the more clearly paradoxical case where everyone is affected by error and is led by that error into conforming with a norm. This focus is dictated primarily by a concern for keeping things simple and manageable.

THE PLAUSIBILITY OF ERROR-DEPENDENCE

These cases of error-dependent norms may seem, on the face of it, to represent logical but very implausible scenarios. For, it may be asked, how could people be led into the egregious sort of error required for the norms to emerge or at least stabilize? Isn't it willful and *ad hoc* to postulate such a rank degree of proneness to error about the values or virtues of others? I shall try to argue that it is not.

Social psychologists have documented a consistent tendency in people's attribution of motives to others that they describe as the fundamental attribution error; I prefer to think of it as a bias, since it may not invariably lead to mistakes. E.E. Jones (1990, p. 138) presents it in the following terms: 'I have a candidate for the most robust and repeatable finding in social psychology: the tendency to see behavior as caused by a stable personal disposition of the actor when it can be just as easily explained as a natural response to more than adequate situational pressure.'

The fundamental attribution bias consists in a preference for explanations of what people do, and of what people say, that emphasizes the contribution of character over context. Let someone do or say something and there will be many possible explanations. Some will suggest that people adapt in very finely tuned ways to differences of circumstances, so that there are no easily predictable patterns in evidence. Others will depict people as possessed of dispositions that are stable across different contexts and that dictate predictable patterns of response: patterns that materialize reliably across quite different sorts of circumstances. The fundamental attribution bias consists in a preference for this second sort of explanation, in which character receives relatively more weight, context relatively less.

The finding about the fundamental attribution bias – and I shall assume that it is a well-documented finding – bears in an obvious way on issues of the kind that arise with non-internalized norms.

Suppose that your drinking companions routinely drink a certain amount and routinely acquiesce in a general acceptance of that level of drinking, perhaps even offering general applause for going that far: we may well expect such applause, given that under the story presented it too can be expected – mistakenly – to earn approval. What more natural explanation of your companions' behavior, then, than that they approve of that level of drinking – in particular, perhaps disapprove of a lower level – and that this approval plays a role in explaining their behavior? To explain what they do in those terms is to project on them a stable complex of attitude and motive. The disposition imputed suggests that regardless of who they are drinking with, they should each be expected to maintain the same level of consumption; it is to downplay the role that circumstances might be expected to play.

Contrast this sort of explanation, however, with that which appeals to the desire of each to be well regarded by others. Under that account, each has to explain the behavior of the others as the product, not of a simple attitude–motive complex, but in terms that give a much larger role to context. Each will take others to be stable of disposition at the high level of seeking the approval of others. But the disposition imputed will be expressed in action in very different ways, depending on differences of circumstances. Let the context be one where others are expected to approve of a high level of drinking, and they will tend to drink to that level. Let it be one where others are expected to disapprove of such drinking, and they will tend to drink less.

The fundamental attribution bias is bound to lead people to explain the presentation of others in the simpler, more context-invariant way. And it is precisely that sort of explanation that each is expected to give of the behavior of others in the story about the fixing of the drinking norm. True, the explanation given turns out to be a mistake. But it is not an implausible explanation to posit. It is the sort of account that is bound to appeal to anyone who is susceptible – as we are all said to be susceptible – to the fundamental attribution bias.

The comments made on this case carry over to the second case of non-internalized norms. Imagine that you are a soldier among soldiers, involved in a series of dangerous military engagements. There is no doubt in your mind but that you and your fellows all approve of courage. Nor is there any doubt about this being a matter of shared awareness. After all, you all talk about courage in the most positive terms, and listen to regular harangues on the topic. So now you find that the others in the ranks with you do indeed behave very courageously. What more natural explanation than that this is due to the fact that they put their lives where their words are: they march to the drum of their values?

This explanation is straightforwardly in line with the fundamental attribution bias, imputing to others a stable disposition – again, a simple attitude–motive complex – that can be expected to produce similar behavior across many fine differences of context. Contrast with that explanation the account that you would have to give of others' behavior, were you to grasp the facts of the case, as my hypothesis presents them. As in the other case, you would posit a stable, high-level disposition – the concern with approval – that is liable to produce quite different behaviors in different contexts. You would downgrade character and upgrade context in a way that runs deeply against the grain of the fundamental attribution bias.

I conclude that in these respects the stories told in illustrating the possibility of error-dependent norms are not at all implausible. The alleged mistakes about the values and virtues of others are precisely the sorts of error that we should expect them to be liable to make, according to received psychological analysis.

But there is a second way in which the stories told may be thought to be implausible. They suppose that people can be by moved by one incentive but can expect at the same time that others will explain their behavior by reference to another. The motive that actually operates, according to those stories, involves the desire to enjoy the approval of others and escape their disapproval. But the motive that agents expect to be ascribed involves a much lower-level, context-insensitive disposition. Is it reasonable to suppose that people could expect others to make that sort of mistake?

I believe it is, again because of the presence of the fundamental attribution bias. The motive people expect to be attributed is the disposition to act in a way that answers to how they are (really or apparently) disposed to approve and disapprove of behavior: in the one case the disposition to drink to the level they make a show of endorsing; in the other the disposition to act courageously after a pattern they clearly admire. As there is no surprise about people's explaining the behavior of others in the erroneous manner described, then, so there should be no surprise about their expecting others to make the same mistake in relation to them. If the fundamental attribution bias is really a feature of human psychology, then it is likely to be a salient feature and one that people are likely to expect others to display.

One final question. On the account given, people explain others' behavior by ascribing a stable, dispositional motive, and they expect others in turn to explain their behavior by reference to a similar motive. But they themselves, according to our account, act on the basis of a pattern of motivation that gives the lie to the notion that low-level, dispositional motives are the more or less ubiquitous sources of action. Does this make the account inconsistent? Or does it at least mean that those to whom the account is applied are inconsistent?

No, it does not. I might consistently think that I am motivated differently from others, that others don't see this, and that actually I am exceptional. Unlike others, so I may feel, I lack the required attitude of approval, or I lack the disposition to act as I approve. But I do of course see the importance of securing approval and so fall back myself on this other motive. On the account offered, we might suggest that people generally think they are different from others in these respects. And that would not be a particularly difficult hypothesis to embrace, given the frequent asymmetry in how people view themselves and others.[1]

To sum up, then, there is no deep implausibility in holding by the assumptions that would predict and explain the appearance of error-dependent norms. The fundamental attribution bias, powerfully supported as it allegedly is, should lead us to expect exactly the pattern of motivational attribution that would account for the presence of such norms.

VARIETIES OF ERROR-DEPENDENT NORM

There are two broad types of error-dependent norms that we should expect in light of the story told so far, one sort exemplified by the drinking case, the other by the case of military courage. The first we may describe as value-mistaken norms, the second as virtue-mistaken norms.

Value-mistaken norms will be liable to emerge only so far as two conditions are fulfilled. The first is that those among whom the norm emerges care greatly for one another's approval; in particular, care enough to be ready to act against their own values for the sake of the approval of others. And the second is that conditions are such as to allow the parties to be mistaken about the one another's values, and so about what they are each likely to approve or disapprove.

The first condition suggests that there will be considerable peer pressure associated with membership of the group in question. And the second implies that members of that group do not come together out of a search on the part of each for those of a common mind: a search for people who share the same values and the same attitudes of approval and disapproval; the group forms on some other basis. These conditions are likely to be fulfilled quite commonly, so that we should not be surprised if there are a variety of value-mistaken norms in place in any society.

Two salient possibilities are worth mentioning. One involves what we might think of norms of corruption: that is, corruption from the point of view of the wider society. Take a group of police officers who have a defensive attitude towards outsiders, expecting them to be somewhat hostile. Membership and acceptance in the group will tend to matter greatly to officers, particularly so far as they expect outsiders not to accept them fully. Given that they do not invariably join the force out of any particular values, there will be room in such a group for members to be unsure about what exactly others care about. In such a scenario it is very possible that a number of value-mistaken norms may emerge or stabilize.

Imagine that someone in the group is seen by others as breaching police rules – that is, the rules imposed by higher authority – in some perhaps not very significant manner. Will any of those others report the breach? Very possibly not, since they are each liable to be afraid of alienating themselves from the offender and his or her friends; and this, even if they each actually disapprove quite strongly of the breach. But suppose now that this pattern of not welching on fellow officers begins to get established as a routine of behavior. As it does, this will suggest to each that others disapprove of welching and approve of turning a blind eye to an individual officer's offences, at least within certain limits. And so we can imagine that a norm of not welching may emerge, with almost everyone conforming, with almost everyone expecting almost everyone to approve of conformity, and with this expectation helping to keep the norm in place. But for all that our story entails, the norm may be value-mistaken in character and so not internalized by the parties. The members of the force may each disapprove of not welching – they may embrace the value of whistle-blowing – and may each keep to the pattern of not welching only out of an erroneous expectation as to how others would respond to whistle-blowing.

If there is a norm of not welching in place among the members of such a police force, of course, then there will be room for the emergence of other value-mistaken norms as well. Suppose that while members of the group think that others disapprove of whistle-blowing, they believe that there are certain limits to what will be tolerated: there are forms of breach such that no one would disapprove of their being publicized. And suppose now that a certain form of breach that goes beyond the ascribed limits begins to emerge in the group – say, one of taking bribes – yet is not exposed by fellow officers. It may be that each is wrong in thinking that this is beyond the limits of tolerance; it may be that the behavior is reported by no one, out of fear of incurring disapproval as a whistle-blower. But so far as there is a general mistake made about the limits of tolerance – surely, a real possibility – each may then be led to think, again mistakenly, that actually the behavior in question is not disapproved of by others, perhaps even that it attracts a degree of approval. The error about attitudes to whistle-blowing can generate other errors too. Value-mistaken norms may multiply and propagate.

The group of police officers imagined exemplifies a range of real-world possibilities. Instead of police officers we might have imagined the lower-level workers in any enterprise, the students in a school, the inmates in a prison, or the members of any professional association. In every such case there will be motives in place that allow for a value-mistaken norm of not whistle-blowing to emerge and, as a result, for the appearance of other value-mistaken norms. These other norms may lead to a tolerance of shirking or bullying or closing ranks against outsiders, even when everyone in the relevant group disapproves of those behaviors.

I do not say, of course, that whenever there is a norm against whistle-blowing, or whenever any of the associated norms prevails, that is because people are mistaken about one another's values. But I do say that even if individuals hold values that would support whistle-blowing and would outlaw a variety of other breaches, those values need not give rise to corresponding norms.

The value-mistaken norms illustrated can be described as norms of corruption, since they support behaviors that fall away from standards that others expect members of the group to honor. But it is worth mentioning that they do not exhaust the possibilities for value-mistaken norms. A second, more or less salient possibility is that norms of correctness, as I will call them, may emerge on the basis of mistaken values. I take the word 'correctness' from the way in which we speak of political correctness, though I believe that norms of correctness may run far beyond the limits of any explicitly political context.

With norms of corruption people are misled by the action or inaction of others into ascribing values that none of them actually endorses. With norms of correctness, they will tend to be misled by the speech or silence of others into making similar mistakes. Suppose that a group of a political or religious or cultural character is established and, as in the earlier sort of case, that it commands great allegiance among members; they each care greatly about belonging. And now imagine how people are likely to respond to the words of some authorities or would-be authorities within the group, when they declare what the attitudes and values of the group are and what they require. Such a declaration will carry influence, so far as no one opposes it. Yet people may each fail to oppose it, not because of sharing the values declared, but because of assuming that others do share them and because of fearing the ostracism that would go with resisting the common line. No one may oppose the declaration, in short, because no one may dare oppose it; no one may think that the risk of being the only dissident voice is worth taking.

Nor is this all. It is also possible in such a case that the person or persons who assume the role of authority and declare the values of the group are not themselves sincere. Just as those who fail to oppose them may not share in the declared values, so the authorities themselves may fail to share in them. The people involved may mistakenly think that others do share the values and may put themselves forward as spokespersons for those values, not out of an attachment to the ideals, but out of a wish to ingratiate themselves with other members of the group.

This possibility is all too easy to envisage. Any number of political and religious and social movements are liable to generate the sort of pressure under which words can engender norms that no one dares to dishonor, even while they are each opposed to the norms in their hearts. Insincerely endorsed words may be cheap for those who utter them; indeed, they may promise a positive reward in the approval that they are expected to earn. And insincerely accepted or unopposed words may be powerful; they may give rise to a cascade of behaviors that no one approves but that everyone displays.

So much for value-mistaken norms, whether of corruption or correctness. The other error-dependent norms that we identified are virtue-mistaken rather than value-mistaken. They arise, not on the basis of an error about what others approve or disapprove, but on the basis of an error about why others display the behavior of which they approve and avoid the behavior of which they disapprove. The error here consists in thinking that others are virtuous – they are disposed to act according to their values – and that it is their virtue rather than any ulterior motive that explains why their actions conform to what they say and think.

Virtue-mistaken norms presuppose that membership and acceptance matter to people just as much as they do in the other case, so that each is loathe to lose the approval of others or earn their disapproval. But it is a matter of common awareness in this case that such and such patterns of behavior are approved of or disapproved of – the values of people in the group are manifest. Here error can kick in, then, not in the perception of how others approve or disapprove, but only in the perception of their motives. Why, however, might it kick in? Why might it be the case that although everyone thinks that others are possessed of the virtue of living up to their values, no one actually has that sort of virtue?

The obvious answer is that while such virtue is a natural disposition to ascribe in explanation of value-conforming behavior – this, in view of the fundamental attribution bias – the value in question is very demanding and is unlikely to be capable of motivating the ordinary run of people, all on its own. In order to identify examples of virtue-mistaken norms, then, we need only reflect on cases where the values that people proclaim – and proclaim sincerely – are really very demanding and are unlikely to have such an imaginative and emotional appeal that they will routinely gird agents against temptation. People will see others generally conforming but will have to struggle against temptation to conform themselves. And when they succeed, if they succeed, that will not be because they are as virtuous as they think others are. It will be because the cost of failure, as they see it, would be too grave to bear: it would consist in being seen, to their shame, as more or less isolated defectors.

The case of military courage exemplifies this structure faithfully. It goes against the grain of human nature, by the testimony of history and introspection, to expose oneself to grievous physical danger; or to do this, at any rate, when there is no immediate goal like that of aiding a comrade in trouble. But in the military context everyone will clearly regard action in the face of such danger as a supreme value and everyone will see others as having enough virtue – enough courage – to be able to honor that value in practice. In such a context, the prospect of being the only one not to act virtuously – the only one not to act as if they had the virtue – will promise ignominy and stigma. It should be no surprise if, under the force of that motive, everyone does indeed act virtuously. No one has the virtue of courage: no one has an attachment to the value that is strong enough to see them through adversity. But, this being the only way to avoid the prospect of a crushing burden of shame, everyone simulates the presence of such virtue and seeks to hide what they wrongly see as their untypical, perhaps unique, cowardice.

The structure that courage exemplifies, according to this story, is liable to be replicated across many different contexts. Take any of the values such that they are universally acknowledged; they are difficult in practice to honor; yet as a matter of fact they are fairly generally respected. In any such case, there will be a possibility that the norm is maintained on a virtue-mistaken basis. There is going to be a question, then, as to how far various norms may not be due to mistakes on people's parts about one another's virtue.

We have focused in this chapter, for simplicity, on cases where error is wholesale rather than coming in degree. There may not be many norms where it is plausible to think that they are virtue-mistaken in that wholesale way but there are likely to be many where such error plays at least a partial role.

Think of values that are commonly proclaimed, whether in society as a whole or in certain groups, such as punctiliousness in making one's tax return, steadfastness in upholding a religious faith, or conscientiousness in preparing oneself for committee deliberations. All of these values make demands that may prove hard to sustain as one is assailed by the temptation to fudge some financial details, to raise doubts about a church's teaching, or to cut corners in reading background material. People may well overcome such temptations by dint of attachment to the relevant value. But there is always a possibility that the real force that enables them to achieve this success is not their natural virtue but the belief that others do have such virtue combined with the desire to avoid the shame of appearing to be more or less isolated deviants.

The examples of value-mistaken and virtue-mistaken norms that we have canvassed in this last section should be sufficient, I hope, to show that error-dependent norms are not only a possibility; it is very likely that some such norms obtain in any society or any grouping. That people conform to norms, then, does not mean that those norms are internalized amongst them: that they internalize the values and the corresponding virtuous dispositions. Many norms may prevail – whether for good or for ill – as a result of the simulated adherence to certain values or the simulated display of certain virtues. The social patterns that obtain among people in aggregate may give only very misleading cues as to the patterns that obtain in their individual souls.[2]

NOTES

1. There is a second fairly plausible hypothesis that would also explain how I could act on one motive but expect to be ascribed another. This is that I am not always aware of how my own motives work. While being sensitive primarily to the forces of approval and disapproval, I may often imagine, whether out of self-ignorance or self-deception, that I am not like this; that I am, in fact, exactly like others in being moved by the same values or the same virtues.
2. This chapter was prompted by some characteristically trenchant queries that Bob Goodin raised about the fact that under the approach taken in Brennan and Pettit (2004), norms need not be internalized.

REFERENCES

Aristotle (1976), *The Nichomachean Ethics*, Harmondsworth: Penguin.

Brennan, G. and P. Pettit (1993), 'Hands Invisible and Intangible', *Synthese*, **94**: 191–225.

Brennan, G. and P. Pettit (2000), 'The Hidden Economy of Esteem', *Economics and Philosophy*, **16**: 77–98.

Brennan, G. and P. Pettit (2004), *The Economy of Esteem: An Essay on Civil and Political Society*, Oxford: Oxford University Press.

Coleman, J. (1990), *Foundations of Social Theory*, Cambridge, Mass: Harvard University Press.

Cooter, R.D. (1994), 'Structural Adjudication and the New Law Merchant: A Model of Decentralized Law', *International Journal of Law and Economics*, **14**: 215–31.

Cooter, R.D. (1996), 'Decentralized Law for a Complex Economy: The Structural Approach to Adjudicating the New Law Merchant', *University of Pennsylvania Law Review*, **144**: 1643–96.

Dharmapala, D. and R.H. McAdams (2001), 'Words that Kill: An Economic Perspective on Hate Speech and Hate Crimes', *University of Illinois Law and Economics Research Papers*, Champaign: Urbana.

Elster, J. (1990), 'Norms of Revenge', *Ethics*, **100**: 862–85.

Elster, J. (1999), *Alchemies of the Mind: Rationality and the Emotions*, Cambridge: Cambridge University Press.

Goffman, E. (1975), *Frame Analysis: An Essay on the Organization of Experience*, Harmondsworth: Penguin Books Ltd.

Hardin, R. (1995), *One for All: The Logic of Group Conflict*, Princeton, NJ: Princeton University Press.

Hart, H.L.A. (1961), *The Concept of Law*, Oxford: Oxford University Press.

Jones, E.E. (1990), *Interpersonal Perception*, New York: Freeman.

Lewis, D. (1969), *Convention*, Cambridge, Mass: Harvard University Press.

Lovejoy, A.O. (1961), *Reflections on Human Nature*, Baltimore: John Hopkins Press.

McAdams, R.H. (1995), 'Cooperation and Conflict: The Economics of Group Status Production and Race Discrimination', *Harvard Law Review*, **108**(5): 1003–84.

McAdams, R.H. (1997), 'The Origin, Development and Regulation of Norms', *Michigan Law Review*, **96** (2): 338–433.

Miller, D.T. and D.A. Prentice (1994), 'Collective Errors and Errors about the Collective', *Personality and Social Psychology Bulletin*, **20**: 541–50.

Miller, D.T. and D.A. Prentice (1996), 'The Construction of Social Norms and Standards', in E.T. Higgins and A.W. Kruglanski (eds), *Social Psychology: Handbook of Basic Principles*, New York: Guilford Press, pp. 799–829.

Nisbett, R.E. and D. Cohen (1996), *Culture of Honor: The Psychology of Violence in the South*, Boulder: Westview Press.

Pettit, P. (1990), '*Virtus Normativa*: A Rational Choice Perspective', *Ethics*, **100**: 725–55; reprinted in P. Pettit (2002), *Rules, Reasons, and Norms*, Oxford: Oxford University Press.

Pettit, P. (1995), 'The Virtual Reality of Homo Economicus', *Monist*, **78**: 308–29. Expanded version in U. Maki (ed.), *The World of Economics*, Cambridge: Cambridge University Press, 2000; reprinted in P. Pettit (2002), *Rules, Reasons, and Norms*, Oxford: Oxford University Press.

Prentice, D.A. and D.T. Miller (1993), 'Pluralistic Ignorance and Alcohol Use on Campus', *Journal of Personality and Social Psychology*, **64**: 243–56.

Schroeder, C.M. and D.A. Prentice (1998), 'Exposing Pluralistic Ignorance to Reduce Alcohol Use Among College Students', *Journal of Applied Social Psychology*, **28**: 2150–80.

Sober, E. and D.S. Wilson (1998), *Unto Others: The Evolution and Psychology of Unselfish Behavior*, Cambridge, Mass: Harvard University Press.

Ullmann-Margalit, E. (1977), *The Emergence of Norms*, Oxford: Oxford University Press.

Winch, P. (1963), *The Idea of a Social Science and Its Relation to Philosophy*, London: Routledge.

8. The world is a table. Economic philosophy stated flatly in terms of rows, columns and cells*

Hartmut Kliemt

INTRODUCTION AND OVERVIEW[1]

Speaking of 'public choice' we do not intend to point out that some 'choice' is taking place in public. This may or may not be the case. Neither do we literally mean that 'the public' is making 'choices'. 'The public' is not naturally a choice-making entity as for instance a person would be (and neither is the state such an entity).[2] Using the term 'public choice' we imply only that there is a (political) process in which results with 'public goods characteristics' emerge.[3] Nevertheless we somehow link our preferences over collective outcomes with choices. Accordingly we tend to speak of 'collective choice' and 'social choice' as if it were clear what those terms mean. But in spite of a huge literature (starting, in a way, with Arrow, 1951, and leading to such works as MacKay, 1980 and Sen, 1970a, 1982/3) it is unclear whether there is such a thing as 'collective or social choice'. In the last resort 'collective choice' is simply a *game or a set of rules* under which *individuals* interact (see on Arrow's approach in a game setting Wilson, 1972). The rules of the game may be changed by choices affecting the rules but strictly speaking the outcome of a play of a game is never chosen, only the moves that make up the play of a game are.[4]

Even in the 'politics as emergent' tradition there is the idea of a 'choice of the rules of the game' (as for instance in Buchanan and Tullock, 1962 and Brennan and Buchanan, 1985). But strictly speaking the rules are emergent, too, and cannot be chosen (see for such a view see Hayek, 1973–79). There is a hiatus between what we as individuals prefer *for* the collectivity and what we as individuals can choose. As Hobbes was well aware (see Hobbes, 1651/1968) in 'foro interno' we may all have good reasons to wish that rules emerge but in 'foro externo' the rules must be brought into existence by individuals who may lack sufficient reasons for taking appropriate actions. Even if there is a unanimous preference for having certain acts performed as part of a 'choreography of play for the game of life' it is in no way certain that the game will be played accordingly (see on inefficient una-nimity Brennan and Lomasky, 1984, or any public goods' provision game with free-riding).

The link between individual intentions for the collectivity, individual actions and collective results is missing. That this is so raises some of the most basic economic philosophy questions. I will deal with them by means of a 'flat earth theory of the economic world'; that is multidimensional philosophical and economic problems will be put very flatly on (or in) 'tables' of two person games. Once stated that 'plainly' in terms of rows, columns and cells some of the problems will simply vanish. But even though most of the economic philosopher's world is flat and can be described in the language of cells, rows, and columns there is something above the plane. There are relationships between preferences *for* the collectivity and indi-viduals' actions (or, more technically speaking, between preferences over outcomes in game forms and moves in game forms) that we still need to understand more fully. But even if we eventually may have to rise above the plane it is worthwhile to explore our tabular world first.

CHOICE, CELLS, ROWS, AND COLUMNS

Consider a two-by-two matrix game-*form* (basically a move structure or the strategic form thereof with outcomes but without preferences) rep-resenting the social interaction of Hartmut and Geoffrey (Table 8.1). Hartmut can choose up or down. Geoffrey can choose left or right. Acting in isolation both have two acts from which to choose. The result of ending up in a cell either emerges or not after all choices have been made. For some reason or other we both might wish to realize any of the set of cells {1,2,3,4}. In pre-play communication we might find out what our wishes are and agree to co-ordinate our choice making according to our inten-tions. Nevertheless, none of us can choose *any of the cells* unilaterally. If a choice in the proper sense of that term can be made only by a person (a personal player) then, since the 'pair' (Hartmut, Geoffrey) is not a person, no cell can be *chosen in the proper sense of the term 'choice'*. Persons

Table 8.1   Game-form A

Geoffrey Hartmut	Left	Right
Up	1	2
Down	3	4

as independent centers of decision making choose 'down' and 'right' but there is *no* 'choice' of '(down, right)' even though the cell corresponding to '(down, right)' would emerge 'down right' as the result of choices of 'down' and of 'right'.

Market games as well as political games are *n*-person games. It is obvious that in *both* cases collective results are not chosen but emerge. In that regard there is no difference between markets and politics. It may be that, as a rule, in collective choice the – or some – collective result is intended whereas in market games the collective result may be entirely unintended. But even in market choice somebody can intend to bring about a collective outcome – for instance if people 'buy American' or buy pollution certificates with the purpose of influencing overall outcomes of markets. But let us avoid getting into *n*-person games prematurely and rather focus on the conditions for 'choosing' a cell in the most basic two by two case. If we do so we have almost no choice but must enter a discussion of a notorious paradox.

LIBERAL PARADOX?

Assume that Geoffrey were a puppet on my, Hartmut's, strings. Then I could not only intend to bring about one of the four possible results. I could do more than creating a necessary condition for its emergence by choosing one of two actions. I could indeed choose between four actions '(up, left), (up, right), (down, left), (down, right)'. I might, say, choose 'down and pull the string such that Geoffrey's arm would move as to bring about right'. I could claim that 'I have chosen' then '(down, right)'. This is a choice in the full sense of a single person being in control. Though it may have involved two co-ordinated actions of mine, it is not a co-ordinated action of two persons. One person serves only as an instrument. So there is in the proper sense of that term a choice of the cell 4 by the *person* that I am. And, since I have full control I could as well choose any other cell.

Assume now that preferences over results are common knowledge among Hartmut and Geoffrey. Hartmut knows that Geoffrey knows that, and so on, and likewise Geoffrey knows that. Let the preferences be of the following (pd) structure:

Hartmut's: $3 >_H 1 >_H 4 >_H 2$
Geoffrey's: $2 >_G 1 >_G 4 >_G 3$

Interpret the choices of 'up', 'down', 'left', 'right', in terms of the following actions:

Up: 'Hartmut reads Lady Chatterley'
Down: 'Hartmut does not read Lady Chatterley'
Left: 'Geoffrey does not read Lady Chatterley'
Right: 'Geoffrey does read Lady Chatterley'

From this we get an interpreted table of the interaction between Geoffrey and Hartmut in our simple two-dimensional world (Table 8.2). If the two of us choose to read or not to read independently of each other's choices then the result might fall into any of the cells in the matrix representation of game B. Being prudish Hartmut, I prefer most to end up in cell 3 where none has to read the book. But if one has to do it I would volunteer to read rather than have Geoffrey in his 60s read the book (cell 1). If Geoffrey cannot be prevented I would rather spare me the necessity of reading *Lady Chatterley's Lover* (cell 4). From my prudish point of view it would be worst if we both were exposed to such tempting literature (cell 2). Of course, Geoffrey, whom age has advanced above conventional morals, sees things in a different light. He would prefer it most if we both read the book (cell 2) but if only one reads it he feels that it would do me good to be exposed to it (cell 1). That, he agrees with me, would be better than him reading the book while I would not (cell 4). Geoffrey obviously deems it more important that I would be stirred up a bit than that he would have the pleasure himself. Finally, from Geoffrey's point of view the worst would be that the pleasure would be forgone entirely since none would read the book (cell 3).

As is well known the preferences described give rise to what Sen called 'the impossibility of a Paretian liberal' (see Sen, 1970b). According to the paradox we cannot both have the right to choose between one pair of cells each and at the same time guarantee Pareto efficiency. According to Sen's presentation of the matter the most minimal right that we can conceivably possess entitles us to choose on behalf of the collectivity between two cells each. More precisely, the collectivity entitles us to fix 'on behalf of the

Table 8.2   Game B

Geoffrey Hartmut	Left: Geoffrey does not read Lady Chatterley	Right: Geoffrey reads Lady Chatterley
Up: Hartmut reads Lady Chatterley	1	2
Down: Hartmut does not read Lady Chatterley	3	4

Preferences: Hartmut: $3 >_H 1 >_H 4 >_H 2$; Geoffrey: $2 >_G 1 >_G 4 >_G 3$

collectivity' the choice of one of the cells from at least one pair of cells as the collectively chosen result.

Granting this conceptualization of a minimal right the paradox unfolds in the following way. Assume, I may choose *for* the collectivity – or make a choice that will be collectively endorsed – between the two cells where I read and where I do not read if Geoffrey does not read, that is, between 1 and 3. Likewise, if I do not read, Geoffrey may choose for the collectivity between cells 3 and 4. Following, for the time being, Sen's original presentation in which implicitly the possibility of both of us reading the book was ruled out – for example since there is merely one copy of it – we can leave out alternative 2 from the set of possible collective results. The choice set is {1,3,4}. The collective choice emerges from pairwise comparisons of alternatives. In this 'social preference conceptualization of rights' (see Sugden, 1994, p. 38) the comparisons are made by authorized agents who as bearers of rights *choose on behalf of the collectivity* and in terms of the Pareto principle.

More specifically, the collectivity grants me the right to choose between the two elements of {1,3} by endorsing my choice as its own 'collective choice of a cell'. I fix the collective choice from the set {1,3} at 3, which rules out 1 as the 'collectively chosen' result. We are unanimous in desiring the choice of 1 from {1,4}. So by the Pareto principle alternative 4 is ruled out. The remaining pairwise comparison concerns the elements of {3,4}. Geoffrey has the right to decide between cells 3 and 4 for the collectivity and will fix the collective choice at 4 which rules out 3. All the alternatives are ruled out by the procedure, none is chosen by it collectively.

This is one variant of the paradox (if a coarse one). But if we insist that only persons can choose then the whole paradox immediately falls to the ground. Though emergent results can be *evaluated* according to the Pareto principle the principle itself cannot fix choices. The construction uses a principle of *evaluation* as if it were in fact *making a choice* (even though there is no choice maker who could single-handedly choose according to the principle).[5]

But this is not the strongest objection. There is a more serious objection to the preceding construction of rights. According to Sen's argument in introducing his *minimal* liberalism it is less demanding to endow the actors with the ability to choose merely between two cells than to be able to choose between more than two cells. But that statement is ambiguous. The ability of an individual to choose single-handedly one cell out of {1,2} is clearly less of an endowment than the ability to choose one element out of {1,2} *and* to choose single-handedly one out of {3,4}. However, the ability of choosing *one single cell* in two cases is completely different from the ability of choosing *one of two classes of cells* from the set of sets {{1,2},{3,4}} even though the latter also involves four cells. As compared with choices of classes of cells – rows or columns of the matrix respectively – it is obvious that the much more demanding assumption is that of being able to discriminate single-handedly between two single cells rather than between two classes of cells. In terms of *choice* in our tabular world what Sen introduced as a weaker or more minimal form of a right is *not* a weaker form. *To be able to choose a cell from one pair of cells rather than to be able to choose one pair of cells from a set of pairs of cells presupposes an amount of control that no individual may have.*[6]

AVOIDING PARADOX

Assume for the sake of the argument that one actor is in fact endowed with the stronger ability to choose between single states rather than classes of states as represented by rows and columns. More specifically assume that I could get again into the position of the puppet master. Then I could and would prevent Geoffrey from reading the book and refrain from reading the book myself. If I could make the choice of a cell, I would choose cell 3. If I could do this in the case of one cell, I should naturally be able to do it in the case of all cells. Then it would clearly not be possible that Geoffrey could have the same faculty for any pair of cells. After I am in control Geoffrey has lost control. There cannot be more than one choice maker. That choice maker would make all choices from the driver's seat, so to say.

However, one might wonder, could it not be true that there is local dictatorship without spreading to all cells? I have the ability to lead Geoffrey along by pulling the strings if it comes to the choice between cells 1 and 3 and he can do the same thing if it comes to the choice between 2 and 4 (however strange it may seem intuitively that Geoffrey could decide on my reading behavior). This assignment of decision rights is obviously viable and implies the following predictions about which results would emerge. Being in state 1 initially, we would end up in state 3 and, being in state 4 initially, we would end up in state 2. Being in state 2 or 4 initially we would stay put. That is the end of it, no paradox implied, or so it seems.

But what if we agree that whenever the Pareto principle applies, Geoffrey is in control? Would he not then transform state 4 into state 1? Obviously, if common knowledge of preferences holds good – as assumed here – Geoffrey would anticipate (old age tends to render us less myopic anyway) that then I would exercise my right and transfer the two of us to cell 3. He would resent that and therefore act strategically in not bringing about state 1. If I were in charge and state 4 applied I would, of course, then bring about state 1 first and then 3. This is an interesting insight about the strategic character of unanimous decisions if the Pareto principle is, so to say, embedded into a structure of rights but it is not a demonstration of paradox. Some kind of full control is necessary if choices of cells are to be made. But if we have that kind of control it is clear what the outcome would be. Either the global dictator fixes the outcome whatever the status quo assumption might be or a local dictator fixes it once the status quo is defined.[7]

Now, as has been argued frequently, if rights are defined in terms of choices between rows and choices between columns, respectively, then individuals could exercise their rights without any problem. Explicating rights in terms of the move structure of a game avoids the preceding paradoxical conclusions. Since there seem no strong arguments to prevent us from using this game form explication of the term 'right' why not use it? Moreover, to explicate rights in terms of rows/columns seems well motivated independently of the aim of avoiding paradox. Rights as we conventionally understand them are related to institutional protections in terms of the rules of the game rather than its emergent outcomes.

Obviously 'the game form conceptualization of rights' is natural and has great merit (for a statement to this effect from scholars close to Sen see Gaertner et al., 1992). The explication of the concept of rights in terms that are independent of outcomes (and preferences over outcomes) seems completely plausible as far as legal institutions are concerned. Still, we *see* (or perceive) outcomes as linked with our behavior and intend to pursue our preferences for collective outcomes through agents in ways different from purely individual strategic action.

AGENTS OF PUBLIC CHOICE AND CONTROL OF CONSEQUENCES

If properly speaking there is no collective choice since besides the ordinary (personal) players there is no player 'the collectivity of all players', no 'we' comprised of all the players in a game, this does not rule out embedding games into other games in which additional players do play a role. Assume that besides Hartmut and Geoffrey there is a third personal actor, Giuseppe. As the name indicates Giuseppe is Italian and therefore naturally in a position to further 'our cause' (or in Italian parlance 'cosa nostra'). To do so Giuseppe is endowed with a big stick. By this realistic change in the rules the little game B that we are playing becomes embedded in a larger game C in which Giuseppe is threatening Hartmut and Geoffrey with sanctions if they do not act according to Giuseppe's will. The new game is broadly as shown in Table 8.3.

Obviously full control is missing if Geoffrey and I are independent centers of decision making. Giuseppe is not pulling strings and we are not merely

Table 8.3 Game C

Time 0. The game begins.
Time 1. Giuseppe shows the stick and announces the cell he wants to be chosen and the sanctions he will allocate.
Time 2. Game B* – with the same game-form as B but due to Giuseppe's presence modified incentives – is played.
Time 3. Giuseppe observes the outcome and the behavior of Hartmut and Geoffrey.
Time 4. Giuseppe allocates rewards and punishments to Hartmut and Geoffrey.
Time 5. The game ends.

puppets on his strings. We can act in ways other than Giuseppe wants us to act. Still, with a sufficiently big stick, Giuseppe, even without strings, is in control in a way neither Geoffrey nor I could be in game B. In a Hobbesian perspective Geoffrey and I are still free. We are independent choice makers in the sub-game B*. Nevertheless, in game C and, for that matter, in B*, Geoffrey and I are not independent centers of decision making in the same sense as we were in game B.[8]

With Giuseppe in the game Geoffrey and I have additional options. We can, for instance, try to influence Giuseppe. In the most simple case – provided he is willing to lend us one – we may whisper in the ear of our (benevolent) despot and he then might decide on making us do what 'we' want to do. We convince Giuseppe that he should bring us into cell 1. He is an independent choice maker, too, of course. But let us, against the grain of public choice, as understood in Virginia and practiced in Italy, assume that Giuseppe's interests are as a matter of fact such that his threats are credible *if and only if* he has been asked by us and promised us to enforce certain courses of action. By threatening both of us with severe punishments if we would deviate from the choice of actions 'up' and 'left', respectively, Giuseppe provides us both with sufficient incentives to act in certain ways. The ways are assigned *to* us *by* us in our 'joint' capacities as agreeing individuals. We might even imagine and want to say that cell 1 is 'chosen' by 'us' – though, of course, through the intervention of Giuseppe.

Note that we had to talk to Giuseppe in the first place. The acts of talking him into something we desired were normal individual 'speech' acts performed by us in our separate individual capacities. In a fully specified game these acts would have to show up as moves. Giuseppe's act of threatening is an act of an individual that would show up in the move structure of the game. Therefore a natural 'reduction' of allegedly collective to individual acts is possible in the case at hand.[9] And a conventional non-cooperative game analysis would inform us about rational strategic action. In the game there is simply no 'we' composed out of the players of the game. There are only Geoffrey, Giuseppe and Hartmut. The game form conceptualization of rights in the spirit of Buchanan's original criticisms of the paradox of liberalism (see Buchanan, 1996, originally written in 1975 but never published) therefore eliminates the paradox of liberalism. It does not come back if public choice is introduced by the presence of an agent like Giuseppe. As long as we focus on the games actually played, the move structure of games says all that is there to say about rights. But if Hartmut and Geoffrey start to *think* about what to choose in terms of cells rather than in terms of rows and columns would that not at least imply something that goes beyond them as individuals? Besides choices and behavior of individuals there are values and perceptions of individuals, and these are as a matter of fact framed in terms other than individual strategic choices.

SEN, SENSIBILITY, AND SENSE

Personal choice makers clearly *think* in terms of a community of choice makers engaging collective action. The image of choosing as collective entities appeals to their sensibilities though it might not make much sense in individual action terms. We all are not impervious to such influences. Like sensibilities in general, 'we'-thinking has some power over our minds and our actions. We simply tend to deliberate in terms of what 'we' as a collective unit rather than several individuals in their separate capacities should do. 'Team reasoning' is a reality even if there are no collectivities choosing as unitary actors.

Even if there is no driver we as passengers on a collective trip imagine that there is one. We see ourselves in the driver's seat, and such imaginations influence where we travel. According to the corresponding reading of the liberal paradox we might use terms like that of a 'right' in this spirit. On this account we are not speaking about respecting spheres of *choice making* when we say that individuals have rights. We are rather addressing issues like that of giving the values of others due *consideration* in our formation of value judgments (or preferences) for the collectivity. 'Rights' of such a kind (consideration rights if you will) enter the *deliberations* of moral persons in different ways than their preferences concerning rights as institutional facts.

Though conceptualizing 'rights' as considerations that enter individuals' formation of value judgments (or preferences) seems less 'natural' than conceptualizing them as institutional rules there are concepts of 'moral rights' as opposed to say 'legal rights' that are not too far off. The non-institutional conceptualization of rights also seems to be close to classical welfare economics and the non-institutional interpretation of the welfare function. According to this view in deliberating the welfare implications of alternative policies, comparisons between persons are made intra-personally by some individual who forms a welfare function for evaluating the welfare of the collectivity from that individual's point of view (on how to induce even inter-personal convergence of the functions see, of course, Harsanyi, 1977). As Prasanta Pattanaik has forcefully argued this leads to what may be called the deliberative as opposed to the institutional interpretation of the Arrow approach (see Pattanaik, 2003). It can be used to make sense of 'trying to express rights in terms of individuals' preferences' (Sugden, 1994, p. 45).[10]

The approach can be stated 'flatly' again in terms of the language of cells, rows and columns of our tabular world. Assume that I intend to form a welfare judgment for the collectivity of (Geoffrey, Hartmut). I wonder how I should order the cells in forming my moral preferences if I subscribe to certain values that go beyond my strictly particular interests. Note that the problem is not anymore which of the cells I should choose. I accept that I cannot literally make that choice. I accept that I can choose only rows. Still, I have values concerning the results. In particular I include in my evaluation of cells not only how the emergence of those cells would affect others but also their wishes and values.

My individual welfare function for the collectivity represents my preferences after taking into account such concerns. Since the modern concept of representative utility is not confined to representing any specific class of motives it is not clear what would distinguish such a function from a 'normal' utility function (and strategic action on behalf of that ethically loaded function).

In one interpretation my welfare function for (Geoffrey, Hartmut) is a 'partial' rather than complete preference representation. It does not represent my preferences all things considered. It exclusively represents my 'ethical preferences' (possibly in the sense of Harsanyi, 1977) for the relevant collectivity of individuals. These ethical preferences are formed from an impartial point of view that takes Geoffrey's preferences along with mine into account.[11] More specifically, assume that my ethical preferences are represented by my welfare function $W_H(.)$ for the collectivity. Likewise Geoffrey's ethical preferences over cells are represented by his welfare function for the collectivity $W_G(.)$. The tabular world that emerges is shown in Table 8.4.

I form my ethical value judgment according to some ethical principles. In particular I grant a *right of equal consideration* to Geoffrey and his evaluation of the world in forming my evaluations. I intend to pass judgment from the point of view of an impartial spectator. In doing so I look at how Geoffrey values states of affairs according to his non-ethical value function

Table 8.4   Game-form D

Geoffrey Hartmut	Left Geoffrey does not read Lady Chatterley	Right Geoffrey reads Lady Chatterley
Up: Hartmut reads Lady Chatterley	$W_H(1)$, $W_G(1)$	$W_H(2)$, $W_G(2)$
Down: Hartmut does not read Lady Chatterley	$W_H(3)$, $W_G(3)$	$W_H(4)$, $W_G(4)$

and then let those non-ethical preferences of his along with my non-ethical preferences enter into the formation of my ethical value function.[12]

Assume that in an anti-utilitarian impulse I want to go beyond 'equal consideration'. I intend to express a more absolute respect for the autonomy of Geoffrey. Rather than merely giving his pre-ethical values equal consideration I render them 'locally' decisive (or decisive in certain regards) in the formation of my ethical preference. In doing so I follow Sen's concept of a right and think that Geoffrey's non-ethical preferences should fix my ethical preference for the collectivity with respect to his reading behavior. I do so regardless of what my own non-ethical preferences are. In forming my ethical preferences I grant him 'a moral right' and therefore do not admit any trade-offs of his with, for instance, my preferences.[13]

Fully respecting Geoffrey's partial preferences in the formation of my impartial ethical preferences has far-reaching consequences. To see which, and to indicate that Geoffrey and I as participants of the interaction do evaluate it from an impartial spectator's or at least some sort of moral point of view, let us take recourse again to that helpful figure Giuseppe. He is to serve as our role model of an impartial spectator now. We imagine being in his shoes when forming our impartial ethical rather than our partial personal value judgments about the cells of the table (otherwise he has no function for our discussion here).

Giuseppe, quite uncharacteristically for an Italian, makes our (that is, Hartmut's and Geoffrey's) values his own in the following way: He wants to respect Hartmut's and Geoffrey's non-ethical preferences over cells in forming his ethical preferences based on the values of the individuals directly concerned. But Giuseppe is not only adopting a so-called moral point of view. As a Sen-type Paretian liberal he intends to do it in a specific 'liberal' way. To see more clearly what is involved here let us go over several alternatives.

Let us start by assuming that Giuseppe adopts a purely formal point of view in interpreting what liberalism requires. At least in one case of one pairwise comparison of end states he intends to follow Hartmut's values in forming his welfare function – let that be the set {1,3}. Likewise he intends to form his own values concerning the ranking of cells in at least one pairwise comparison by making Geoffrey's judgment his own – let that be the set{2,4}. So Giuseppe has granted 'moral rights' to both of us. He forms his ethical preferences in two cases – one for each person – according to the individual's values without admitting any trading off or comparison with the values of the other. Clearly, whatever the preferences of Hartmut and Geoffrey might be, the formal requirement could be fulfilled. Of course, Giuseppe's value order is incomplete. Therefore, Giuseppe, if he could choose one state single-handedly, would not know which to choose. But that he, according to his incomplete ethical preferences, does not know what to choose from the full set of alternatives is not paradoxical. After all, we are discussing evaluations rather than choices here.

In a formal way Giuseppe fulfills the requirements of Sen's minimal liberalism. However, from a substantial point of view Giuseppe's values concerning the pure form of value formation would not be well in line with what we think is liberal. According to substantial rather than purely formal considerations we would assume that a liberal Giuseppe would let Geoffrey decide on his reading, and likewise Hartmut. The Paretian liberal Giuseppe's welfare function should own Hartmut's orderings in the pairwise comparison of alternatives (1, 3) and (2, 4). Likewise Giuseppe's welfare function should own Geoffrey's value ordering in pairwise comparisons of (1, 2) and (3, 4) respectively if he believes that Geoffrey's own reading given the reading behavior of Hartmut should be decisive. Due to Hartmut's values Giuseppe should rank 3 before 1 and 4 before 2. Likewise, due to Geoffrey's values Giuseppe intends to order 2 before 1 and 4 before 3. From this we get immediately that from his ethical point of view Giuseppe ranks (4 before 3 and 3 before 1) as well as (4 before 2 and 2 before 1). Since Giuseppe is a *rational individual* applying transitivity seems natural. In both cases we get '4 before 1'. However, the Pareto principle brings Giuseppe immediately back to '1 before 4'. It seems that, in the case at hand, Giuseppe cannot form a consistent ethical preference or *value order* on the basis of the individual orders.

The implied criticism concerning the coherence of Giuseppe's Paretian liberalism might be read as attacking the intention of reducing himself to a mere accountant of other individuals' values. This objection echoes one of the fundamental Rawlsian criticisms of utilitarianism. According to this a moral person may not give up her moral autonomy in forming value judgments. The utilitarian is wrong in making his value judgments for the community a function of the individuals' value judgments. The own moral value judgments of a morally autonomous person must not be completely subservient to the value judgments of others. It is morally mistaken to put oneself under a constitution of forming value judgments that takes over as own the judgments of others whatever those judgments may be. The moral autonomy of the individual who forms a personal moral welfare function for a collectivity cannot be given up completely. And, therefore, the welfare function of an autonomous moral person cannot be a *function* of individual evaluations.

However, as sound as such a general criticism in particular of utilitarianism may be otherwise, in the present case we might well say that the dimensions of value for which Giuseppe will make Hartmut's and Geoffrey's values his own are singled out according to moral judgments of Giuseppe. He decided in a prior moral judgment that he should follow individuals' value orderings along the dimensions he singled out *morally* as legitimate concerns solely of the individuals themselves. And in view of the substantial issues involved there is a good moral reason – from the point of view of 'ethical liberalism' – for Giuseppe to make his own ethical value judgment a function of the value judgments of the two individuals directly concerned. What concerns only them taken separately he wants to let them decide for themselves. So let us look into a substantive, as opposed to the preceding purely formal, interpretation of what liberalism requires. If Giuseppe wants to own the individuals' values over their own-reading-dimensions in forming his ethical preference the situation would be the following: since, if Geoffrey reads, I prefer not to read, Giuseppe should adopt my preference and ethically prefer $4 >_{Giu} 2$ (Giuseppe thinks that my non-ethical preference should *ceteris paribus* fix his ethical preference), likewise we get $3 >_{Giu} 1$ for Geoffrey's given behavior of not reading since in that case I also prefer not to read. Analogously for Geoffrey's case we get $2 >_{Giu} 1$ and $4 >_{Giu} 3$. With transitivity the result $4 >_{Giu} 1$ is obvious. But that result is not in line with the Pareto principle which requires that Giuseppe would endorse $1 >_{Giu} 4$.

Before one might say that then as good liberals we should simply let go of the Pareto principle, we should follow Gibbard's lead to see that this would not help either. If Giuseppe faces Hartmut and Geoffrey with non-ethical preferences other than the preceding pd preferences he should still be willing to respect individual reading preferences for the same moral reason that led him to single out those dimensions as individuals' personal concerns. Assume that these preferences are $1 >_H 4 >_H 2 >_H 3, 3 >_G 2 >_G 1 >_G 4$. If Giuseppe wants to own these in his own ethical preferences in the same *ceteris paribus* way as before, then using transitivity $1 >_{Giu} 3 >_{Giu} 4_{Giu} >_{Giu} 2 >_{Giu} > 1$ immediately emerges.

This shows that there is a problem for what may be called '*value or deliberative liberalism*'. There is no welfare function that could represent this kind of liberalism for all profiles of individual non-ethical preferences. The ethical preferences to be represented by the welfare function may become inconsistent. Inconsistency may emerge if the ethical order is to be dictated 'locally' by individual orders. The latter must be accepted by a 'value liberal' who understands the basic principles of liberalism as Sen. At least for some evaluations he should assume that they are only individual concerns. That is, *when forming his liberal welfare judgments for the society at large the deliberative liberal should own the values of several individuals in his own judgments whatever else the non-ethical values of individuals may be.*

The preceding concept of value liberalism is strictly axiological rather than institutional. According to this argument a variant of the paradox liberalism emerges within value or deliberative liberalism. In deliberative liberalism the evaluation of cells is the goal. Single cells are ordered. Therefore the basic argument that cells cannot be chosen does not matter. The deliberative liberal intends to take other individuals' values into account in a specific manner when forming his value judgments. Sen's approach shows that this is not a viable way of forming value judgments.

The meta-ethical relativist – that is, the typical economist – cannot intend to endorse in his own judgments those of the individuals concerned and at the same time insist on Pareto efficiency. The specific combination of evaluative relativism and Paretianism that characterizes much of the implicit ethics of welfare economics is indeed troubled by Sen's paradox. So, by way of conclusions, let us (re-)turn to the two basic questions: first, is the paradox emerging within value liberalism of any relevance for institutional or political liberalism and, second, on a more general plane, what are the implications if constitutional political economy is correctly interpreted as an effort to influence constitutional preference formation rather than to influence (non-existent) constitutional *choice*?

CONCLUSIONS

To start with the first question, the 'natural account' of liberalism is not deliberative or ethical but rather institutional and political. Traditionally we are discussing liberal institutions rather than liberal ways of evaluating institutions. The actual 'rules of the game' and its predicted outcomes are center stage. We focus on the game form plus individual preferences as an object of evaluation rather than on 'the constitution of the evaluation'. And there are good reasons to stick to this even if we agree that constitutions cannot strictly speaking be chosen. For, if constitutions are not chosen but emerge in higher order games then, trivially, constitutions are the outcomes of games not options chosen in a game. As outcomes constitutions correspond to the cells of the matrix in our tabular world.

Table 8.5   Game-form A

Geoffrey Hartmut	Left	Right
Up	1	2
Down	3	4

Even more specifically, assume that making a choice affecting the constitutional rules of a game that they have to play afterwards Hartmut and
Geoffrey can again choose 'up' or 'down', 'left' or 'right' respectively.
According to these four choices four different constitutions emerge. The
game form is shown in Table 8.5. But now the alternatives are to be interpreted as, say,

1: Liberal democracy
2: Liberal aristocracy
3: Benevolent dictatorship
4: Anarchy

One of those games is fixed by the choices on the constitution-creating
game and the post-constitutional preferences that are expected to apply.
The constitutional game is a higher order game that leads to these results.
More technically speaking the results are actually sub-games and the individuals in the higher order game order those sub-games according to some
constitutional preference or other.

In the evaluative interpretation of his approach Sen would have to say
that liberalism concerns the question of how to rank order constitutions
(note that 'one level up' the games to be rank ordered correspond to the
cells). This implies that liberalism as understood by Sen is not a value judgment concerning the structure of the games 1, 2, 3, 4. The games 1, 2, 3, 4
are not deemed either 'liberal' or 'non-liberal'. What is liberal or not is the
form of the personal welfare function or the way, mode or procedure
according to which the alternatives, that is the games, are ranked by each
individual evaluator.

Normative constitutional political economists are interested in the games
themselves whereas deliberative collective choice talks (one level up) about
a 'liberal evaluation' of the games. Or more succinctly, where – in the deliberational interpretation – Sen deals with the 'liberal nature' of the *evaluation*
of games, the constitutional political economist is interested in the 'liberal
nature' of the games themselves. In the interpretation suggested here,
Sen discusses (one level up or in the game where the outcomes are games)
the *form* of rank ordering games (game forms) as accomplished by some

representative individual whereas the normative constitutional political economist discusses the more or less 'liberal' character of the games that are rank ordered.

Accepting that some kind of moral or ethical liberalism may express itself by the willingness to incorporate the value judgments of others into one's own value judgments there may be a *moral* problem of the kind of the so-called liberal paradox. The moral evaluator cannot own other individuals' values and the Pareto principle (under conditions of universal domain of preferences) and by the pursuit of these twin aims express her or his respect of the moral values of other persons. But, to repeat, this variant of 'moral liberalism' does not yield a plausible interpretation of political liberalism. In sum, *in political liberalism the objects of liberal evaluation are constitutions – that are liberal or illiberal – whereas in Sen's deliberational framework it is the evaluation – the procedure of how the personal value judgment is formed – that is liberal, not the constitutions so evaluated.*

The second question raises some rather deep issues for normative constitutional political economy. It seems that an evaluative or deliberative interpretation not only of Sen's approach but also of normative constitutional political economy is implied if constitutions cannot be chosen. After all, by assumption of constitutional political economy, only persons can choose and therefore constitutions as collective outcomes ('cells') are not chosen but emerge in a higher order game.

As long as we evaluate the world based on the consequences brought about by plays of the game of life, our evaluation of cells matters. But we cannot choose what we value – at least not single-handedly. The relationship between preferences over outcomes and over actions is necessarily indirect. Since we cannot choose between cells we do not directly express our preferences concerning cells in our *choices* (unless, of course, we have for example row or column choices with identical results and thus our co-players are mere dummies that cannot exert any causal influence on results).

Totally independently of the explication of liberalism and rights the issue of how to construe that players of a game intend to act in agreement, that they intend to act concertedly rather than strategically, must be better understood. Collective results in one sense always are emergent. But they do not emerge in unintended ways but are intended to emerge. We participate in collective interaction in a way that goes beyond exerting individual strategic influences in bringing about collective results. Though there are some promising first steps towards linking preferences *for* the collectivity with choices under its rules as by acts of 'expressive voting' (see of course Brennan and Lomasky, 1993) economic philosophy must still find ways to provide the missing link between preferences for the collectivity and individual action, between preferences over outcomes and non-strategic behavior in games.

NOTES

* Since Geoffrey Brennan worked on the 'economy of esteem' let me say that this chapter in honor of his 60th birthday is hopefully uneconomical in expressing philosophical esteem. Since I am approaching 60 myself I tend to feel with the elderly rather than with the young and smart. Therefore I chose a topic which tends to confuse the formal wizards while putting a premium on experience and on daring to state things flatly and plainly.

1. In a way this chapter is an extended response to a beautifully clear comment by Breyer (1996). Except for one point about decisiveness I agree with Friedrich (including his diagnosis of my own errors). But contrary to Sen (1996) I insist that the riddle why the 'paradox of liberalism' could be taken seriously as a problem of *political or institutional* liberalism needs explanation since it is so obviously irrelevant for institutional liberalism. Sen has spread confusion by hijacking the term 'liberalism' for his welfare economic and ethical purposes which are quite alien to the institutional issues discussed in political liberalism but there are nevertheless interesting issues here.

2. The original copper engraving on Hobbes' Leviathan is showing a 'corporate actor', a man formed 'out of' individuals (little men). Leviathan – incidentally in the biblical use a symbol of evil – is holding the insignia of sovereign power. The corporate person picture is, as Hobbes was well aware, a metaphor, but to refer to it as a metaphor does not mean that the corporate actor vision would be useless; see for examples to the contrary de Jasay (1998) and Vanberg (1982).

3. For the public at large there is no rivalry in consuming its outcomes nor can any of its members in general exclude themselves from the mixed blessings of the political process.

4. If the term 'collective choice' has characteristics of a systematically misleading expression in Gilbert Ryle's sense (see Ryle, 1931–32) are there explications of the concept that are not systematically misleading?

5. The preceding deficiency of the original argument could conceivably be healed since the collectivity could make either of the two individuals its agent under such circumstances (such arguments will be discussed below).

6. Though I agree with almost everything in Sugden's excellent discussions of the theme I think that it is not the effort to express 'rights in terms of individuals' preferences' (Sugden, 1994, p. 45) that is most mistaken in Sen's original presentation. As I will argue below there is a way to make sense of this conceptualization. The assumption that cells can be chosen is wrong and misleading and not a weak one.

7. Note that local dictators whose choice sets have a common alternative cannot be meaningfully defined since then they could not be dictators concerning the common alternative.

8. In Rousseau's terms Giuseppe can 'force us to be free' meaning to bring about what we would want to be chosen but cannot, due to a lack of control or 'positive freedom', individually bring about.

9. To avoid hen and egg problems in triggering Giuseppe, the same would apply if we would construe our example as Geoffrey contracting with Giuseppe that he, Giuseppe, will threaten him, Geoffrey, into choosing 'left' on condition that I have contracted with Giuseppe that he, Giuseppe, will enforce my choosing 'up' on condition that Geoffrey contracted in the appropriate way with Giuseppe as enforcer.

10. Sudgen, of course, goes on to say that this is where 'the social preference conceptualization goes wrong'; whereas I try to defend it as a possible interpretation of 'liberalism'.

11. They might, of course, enter the formation of all things considered preferences, as for instance equity concerns in some recent economic approaches such as, for example, Bolton and Ockenfels (2000).

12. Note that the preferences borrowed from game B must be partial ones. They are not representing the ordering 'all things considered', for the ethical preferences are still not considered then. Likewise, once the welfare functions of Hartmut and Geoffrey would represent our preferences 'all things considered' then the game-form would turn into a fully specified game.
13. An institutional liberal would focus on the rules of the game that fix the relative borders of spheres. That route was taken in Buchanan in a re-interpretation of the Pareto principle in institutional terms of unanimity. By this move rights as entitlements to fix what is not subject to voting, and voting as entitlements to make the choice of a vote, are of the same kind too. They are all about the rules of the game rather than about preferences concerning the outcomes of the game and their evaluation.

REFERENCES

Arrow, Kenneth J. (1951), *Social Choice and Individual Values*, New York: Wiley.
Bolton, Gary and Ockenfels, Axel (2000), 'ERC: A theory of equity, reciprocity and competition', *American Economic Review*, **90**, 166–93.
Brennan, H. Geoffrey and Lomasky, Loren (1984), 'Inefficient unanimity', *Journal of Applied Philosophy*, **1**(1), 151–63.
Brennan, H. Geoffrey and Lomasky, Loren E. (1993), *Democracy and Decision*, Cambridge: Cambridge University Press.
Brennan, Harold Geoffrey and Buchanan, James McGill (1985), *The Reason of Rules*, Cambridge: Cambridge University Press.
Breyer, Friedrich (1996), 'Comment on the papers by J.M. Buchanan and by A. de Jasay and H. Kliemt', *Analyse & Kritik*, **18**(1), 148–52.
Buchanan, James M. (1996), 'An ambiguity in Sen's alleged proof of the impossibility of a Pareto Liberal', *Analyse & Kritik*, **18**(1), 118–25.
Buchanan, James M. and Gordon Tullock (1962), *The Calculus of Consent*, Ann Arbor: University of Michigan Press.
de Jasay, Anthony (1998), *The State*, Indianapolis: Liberty Fund.
Gaertner, Wulf, Suzumura, Kotaro and Pattanaik, Prasanta K. (1992), 'Individual rights revisited', *Economica*, **59**, 161–77.
Harsanyi, John C. (1977), *Rational Behavior and Bargaining Equilibrium in Games and Social Situations*, Cambridge: Cambridge University Press.
Hayek, Friedrich August v. (1973–79), *Law, Legislation and Liberty: A New Statement of the Liberal Principles of Justice and Political Economy*, London and Henley: Routledge & Kegan Paul.
Hobbes, Thomas (1651/1968), *Leviathan*, Harmondsworth: Penguin.
MacKay, Alfred F. (1980), *Arrow's Theorem. The Paradox of Social Choice. A Case Study in the Philosophy of Economics*, New Haven: Yale University Press.
Pattanaik, K. Prasanta (2003), *Little and Bergson on Arrow's Concept of Social Welfare*, Riverside, CA 92521, USA.
Ryle, Gilbert (1931–32), 'Systematically misleading expressions', *Proceedings of the Aristotelian Society*, **XXXII**, 139–70.
Sen, Amartya K. (1970a), *Collective Choice and Social Welfare*, San Francisco et al.: Elsevier Science Publishing.
Sen, Amartya K. (1970b), 'The impossibility of a Paretian Liberal', *Journal of Political Economy*, **78**, 152–7.
Sen, Amartya K. (1982/3), *Choice, Welfare and Measurement*, Oxford: Basil Blackwell.

Sen, Amartya K. (1996), 'Rights: formulation and consequences', *Analyse & Kritik*, **18**(1), 152–70.

Sugden, Robert (1994), 'The Theory of Rights', in Horst Siebert (ed.), *The Ethical Foundations of the Market Economy*, Tübingen: Mohr, pp. 31–53.

Vanberg, Viktor (1982), *Markt und Organisation. Individualistische Sozialtheorie und das Problem Korporativen Handelns*, Tübingen: Mohr.

Wilson, Robert (1972), 'The game-theoretic structure of Arrow's general possibility theorem', *Journal of Economic Theory*, **5**, 14–20.

Appendix: list of major works by Geoffrey Brennan

BOOKS

The Power to Tax: Analytical Foundations of a Fiscal Constitution, Cambridge: Cambridge University Press, 1980 (with James M. Buchanan).

The Reason of Rules: Constitutional Political Economy, New York: Cambridge University Press, 1985 (with James M. Buchanan).

Democracy and Decision: the Pure Theory of Electoral Preference, New York: Cambridge University Press, 1993 (with Loren Lomasky).

Democratic Devices and Desires, Cambridge: Cambridge University Press, 2000 (with Alan Hamlin).

The Economy of Esteem, Oxford: Oxford University Press, 2004 (with Philip Pettit).

JOURNAL ARTICLES

'Pareto Optimal Redistribution: The Case of Malice and Envy', *Journal of Public Economics*, (1972), 173–83.

'Pareto Optimal Redistribution Reconsidered', *Public Finance Quarterly*, (1973), 147–68 (with Cliff Walsh).

'Pareto Optimal Redistribution: The Non-Altruistic Dimension', *Public Choice*, (1973), 43–61.

'The Distributional Implications of Public Goods', *Econometrica*, (1976), 391–400.

'Pareto-Desirable Redistribution-in-Kind: An Impossibility Theorem', *American Economic Review*, (1977), 987–90 (with Cliff Walsh).

'Towards a Tax Constitution for Leviathan', *Journal of Public Economics*, (1977), 255–75 (with James M. Buchanan).

'A Monopoly Model of Public Goods Provision: The Uniform Pricing Case', *American Economic Review*, **71**(1981), 196–206 (with Cliff Walsh).

'Revenue Implications of Money Creation Under Leviathan', *American Economic Review*, **71**(1981), 347–51 (with James M. Buchanan).

'The Normative Purpose of Economic Science', *International Review of Law and Economics*, **1**(1981), 155–66 (with James M. Buchanan).

'An Economic Theory of Military Tactics: Methodological Individualism at War', *Journal of Economic Behavior and Organization*, **3**(3) (1982), 225–42 (with Gordon Tullock).

'Predictive Power and the Choice Among Regimes', *Economic Journal*, **93** (March 1983), 89–105 (with James M. Buchanan).

'Government Growth and Resource Allocation: The Nebulous Connection', *Oxford Economic Papers*, (1983), 351–65 (with Jonathan Pincus).

'On Monopoly Price', *Kyklos*, **36**(4) (1983), 538–51 (with James M. Buchanan and Dwight Lee).

'Institutional Aspects of Merit Goods Analysis', *Finanzarchiv*, **4** (1983) (with Loren Lomasky).

'Inefficient Unanimity', *Journal of Applied Philosophy*, **1**(1) (1984), 151–63 (with Loren Lomasky).

'Voter Choice and the Evaluation of Political Alternatives: A Critique of Public Choice', *American Behavioral Scientist*, **28**(2) (1984), 185–201 (with James M. Buchanan).

'The Impartial Spectator Goes to Washington: Towards a Smithian Theory of Electoral Politics', *Economics and Philosophy*, **I**(2) (1985), 207–29 (with Loren Lomasky).

'Restrictive Consequentialism', *Australasian Journal of Philosophy*, **64**(4) (December 1986) (with Philip Pettit).

'Methodological Individualism Under Fire', *Journal of Economic Behavior and Organisation*, **8** (1987), 627–35.

'The Logic of Electoral Preference', *Economics and Philosophy*, **3** (1987), 131–8 (with Loren Lomasky).

'Is Public Choice Immoral?', *Virginia Law Review*, **74**(2) (1988), 179–89 (with James M. Buchanan).

'Unveiling the Vote', *British Journal of Political Science*, **20** (1990), 311–33 (with Philip Pettit).

'An Implicit Contracts Theory of Inter-governmental Grants', *Publius: The Journal of Federalism*, **20** (1990), 129–44 (with J.J. Pincus).

'Bi-Cameralism and Majoritarian Equilibrium', *Public Choice*, **74**(2) (1992), 169–80 (with Alan Hamlin).

'Invisible and Intangible Hands', *Synthese*, **94** (1993), 191–225 (with Philip Pettit).

'Rationalising Parliamentary Systems', *Australian Journal of Political Science*, **28** (1993), 443–57 (with Alan Hamlin).

'The Separation of Powers: a Revisionist View', *Journal of Theoretical Politics*, **6**(3) (1994), 345–68 (with Alan Hamlin).

'Finite Lives and Social Institutions', *Kyklos*, **47**(4) (1994), 551–72 (with Hartmut Kliemt).

'Economizing on Virtue', *Constitutional Political Economy*, **6** (1995), 35–56 (with Alan Hamlin).

'Constitutional Political Economy: The Political Economy of Homo Economicus?', *Journal of Political Philosophy*, **3**(3) (1995), 280–303 (with Alan Hamlin).

'Economical Constitutions', *Political Studies*, **XLIV**(3) (1996), 605–19 (with Alan Hamlin).

'A Minimalist Theory of Inter-Governmental Grants', *Journal of Public Economics*, **61** (1996), 229–46 (with Jonathan Pincus).

'Expressive Voting and Electoral Equilibrium', *Public Choice*, **95** (1998), 149–75 (with Alan Hamlin).

'On Political Representation', *British Journal of Political Science*, **29** (1999), 109–27 (with Alan Hamlin).

'The Hidden Economy of Esteem', *Economics and Philosophy*, **16** (2000), 77–98 (with Philip Pettit).

'Is There a Duty to Vote?', *Social Philosophy and Policy*, **17** (2000), 62–86 (with Loren Lomasky).

'Paying for Politics', *Nomos*, **XLII** (2000), 55–74 (with Alan Hamlin).

'Bargaining over Beliefs', *Ethics*, **111**, January (2001), 256–77 (with Robert Goodin).

'Republican Liberty and Resilience', *The Monist*, **84**(1) (2001), 47–62 (with Alan Hamlin).

'Collective Coherence?', *International Review of Law and Economics*, **21** (2001), 197–211.

'Five Rational Actor Accounts of the Welfare State', *Kyklos*, **54** (2001), 213–33.

'The Dubious Ethics of Debt Default', *Public Finance Review*, **30**(6) (2002), 546–61 (with Giuseppe Eusepi).

'Expressive Constitutionalism', *Constitutional Political Economy*, **13**(4) (2002), 299–311 (with Alan Hamlin).

'Power Corrupts, but can Office Ennoble?', *Kyklos*, **55**(2) (2002), 157–78 (with Philip Pettit).

'Trust in the Shadow of the Courts', *Journal of Institutional and Theoretical Economics*, **159** (2003), 16–36 (with H. Kliemt and W. Guth).

'Life in the Putty-Knife Factory', *American Journal of Economics and Sociology*, **63**(1) (2004), 75–104.

'Analytic Conservatism', *British Journal of Political Science*, **34**(4), October (2004), 675–91 (with Alan Hamlin).

'E-reputation and E-esteem', *Analyse und Kritik*, **26** (2004), 139–57 (with Philip Pettit).

Index